A modern take on the classic kitchen timesaver

THE NEW
PRESSURE
COOKER
COOKBOOK

MORE THAN
200
MODERN, EASY RECIPES
FOR TODAY'S KITCHEN

adamsmedia
AVON, MASSACHUSETTS

Published by
Adams Media, a division of F+W Media, Inc.
57 Littlefield Street, Avon, MA 02322. U.S.A.
www.adamsmedia.com

Contains material adapted from *The Everything® Pressure Cooker Cookbook* by Pamela Rice Hahn, copyright © 2009 by F+W Media, Inc., ISBN 10: 1-4405-0017-7, ISBN 13: 978-1-4405-0017-6; *The Everything® Healthy Pressure Cooker Cookbook* by Laura D.A. Pazzaglia, copyright © 2012 by F+W Media, Inc., ISBN 10: 1-4405-4186-8, ISBN 13: 978-1-4405-4186-5; and *The Everything® Vegetarian Pressure Cooker Cookbook* by Amy Snyder and Justin Snyder, copyright © 2010 by F+W Media, Inc., ISBN 10: 1-4405-0672-8, ISBN 13: 978-1-4405-0672-7.

ISBN 10: 1-4405-9749-9
ISBN 13: 978-1-4405-9749-7
eISBN 10: 1-4405-9750-2
eISBN 13: 978-1-4405-9750-3

Printed in the United States of America.

10 9 8 7 6 5 4 3 2 1

Library of Congress Cataloging-in-Publication Data

The new pressure cooker cookbook: more than 200 modern, easy recipes for today's kitchen.
Avon, Massachusetts: Adams Media, [2016]
Includes index.
LCCN 2016005641 (print) | LCCN 2016013166 (ebook) | ISBN 9781440597497 (pb) | ISBN 1440597499 (pb) | ISBN 9781440597503 (ebook) | ISBN 1440597502 (ebook) |
LCSH: Pressure cooking. | LCGFT: Cookbooks.
LCC TX840.P7 N57 2016 (print) | LCC TX840.P7 (ebook) | DDC 641.5/87--dc23
LC record available at http://lccn.loc.gov/2016005641

Always follow safety and commonsense cooking protocol while using kitchen utensils, operating ovens and stoves, and handling uncooked food. If children are assisting in the preparation of any recipe, they should always be supervised by an adult.

Cover design by Frank Rivera.
Cover image © Marianne Oliva/123RF.
Interior images © iStockphoto.com.

This book is available at quantity discounts for bulk purchases.
For information, please call 1-800-289-0963.

Contents

Introduction

It's not your grandmother's pressure cooker any more. While you might be thinking of that huge cast-iron monster from your childhood, modern cutting-edge pressure cookers are sleek, efficient, and easy to operate. In fact, the pressure cooker makes preparing a meal easier, cutting down cooking time from hours to minutes. And, because it seals in essential vitamins and minerals, pressure cookers turn out healthier, better-tasting food that's perfect when you're on the go.

Today's pressure cookers are versatile too, whether you're making a hearty breakfast or a delicious dessert. Home cooks are using them to turn out everything from Hash Browns to Duck in Orange Sauce to Spiced Chocolate Cake. And that's not all! With *The New Pressure Cooker Cookbook* at your side, you can serve family and friends delicious Pesto Chicken or some Beer BBQ Pork Sliders with Apple. Vegetarian? No problem. Whip up some Risotto Primavera or Herb and Quinoa Stuffed Tomatoes. And to top off the meal, try a Lemon Cheesecake or a tasty Crème Caramel.

If you've been holding back because you're not sure how to use a pressure cooker or just don't have much experience cooking, don't worry. In Chapter 1 you'll learn how pressure cookers work, the easiest and safest ways to use them, and how to take care of them. You'll also find a list of cooking terms and what they mean—which will help you easily navigate these and other recipes.

So whether you're getting ready for a party or sitting down to a quiet dinner, get ready to choose from more than 200 fresh, flavorful dishes that will make your mouth water!

CHAPTER 1

Pressure Cooker Primer

Pressure cookers cook food up to 70 percent faster than conventional methods. Steam trapped in the pot builds up pressure, which creates a hotter cooking temperature. The pressure bears down on the surface of the liquid, which isn't able to break down the molecules to create more steam; this produces more heat. The end result is that the pressure raises the boiling point. The tight seal on the cooker also helps seal in vitamins and minerals and prevents the cooker from boiling dry during the cooking process.

A Brief History of Pressure Cookers

Pressure cookers have been around since the seventeenth century and were an essential part of American kitchens in the 1940s, 1950s, and 1960s. In the 1970s, however, pressure cooker popularity in the United States declined as many cooks switched to microwave ovens. Europeans, on the other hand, tended to rely on pressure cookers as their preferred way to fix food quickly.

Today's improved pressure cookers usually feature a stationary pressure regulator that's either a fixed weight or a spring valve. The pressure regulator keeps the pressure even in the cooker by occasionally releasing a burst of steam. The pressure regulator also provides an easy way to quick-release the pressure at the end of the pressure cooking time; this is usually done by pressing a button or flipping a pressure release switch.

New pressure cookers have backup pressure release mechanisms that prevent the excess pressure accidents that were associated with older models. They also have safety features that cause the lid to remain locked into place until after all of the pressure has been released.

Equipment Considerations

Your cooking equipment can make a difference in how easy it is to prepare foods. Buy the best you can afford. Better pan construction equals more even heat distribution, which translates to reduced cooking time and more even cooking.

Food will burn more easily in an inexpensive pan with a thinner pan bottom. How well your cooking pan conducts the heat will make a difference in how high you set the burner temperature. With some practice, you'll soon learn the perfect heat settings for your pressure cooker: It might take a medium-high setting to sauté food in an inexpensive pressure cooker and a lot more stirring to prevent the food from burning, but you can accomplish the same task in a heavier pan when it's over medium heat, and with less frequent stirring.

On the flip side, a heavier pan will retain the heat longer once it's removed from the burner than will an inexpensive one, so to prevent it from overcooking, food cooked to perfection in a heavier pan must be moved to a serving dish more quickly. This is especially true of foods like gravy that tend to thicken the longer they sit; gravy can turn from a

succulent liquid to one big lump if it stays on the heat too long.

Pressure Release Methods

The ways pressure is released from the pressure cooker are:

* The natural release method, which refers to turning off the heat under the pressure cooker and either removing the pan from the heat or letting the pan remain on the burner, and then waiting until the pressure cooker has cooled sufficiently for all of the pressure to be released.
* The quick release method, which refers to using the valve on the pressure cooker to release the pressure.
* The cold water release method, which occurs when the pan is carried to the sink and cold water from the tap is run over the lid of the pressure cooker (but not over the valve!) until the pressure is released.

DON'T OVERFILL

Read the instruction manual that came with your pressure cooker. Never exceed the fill line for your pressure cooker; adjust the recipe or prepare it in two batches if you need to. Overfilling the pressure cooker can cause it to explode, so be careful!

The cold water release method isn't suggested in any of the recipes in this book; however, if you find that your pressure cooker retains too much heat after the quick release method when you prepare foods that only require a short cooking time—like certain vegetables, risotto, or polenta—try using the cold water release method the next time you fix that food.

Explanation of Cooking Methods

Cooking terms that you'll encounter in this book are:

Bain-marie, or water bath

This is a method used to make custards and steamed dishes by surrounding the cooking vessel with water; this helps maintain a more even cooking temperature around the food.

Baking

This involves putting the food in a preheated oven; the food cooks by being surrounded by the hot, dry air of your oven. In the pressure cooker, foods that are traditionally baked (like a cheesecake, for example) are baked in a covered container that's placed on a rack submerged in water. The water in the bottom of the pressure cooker creates the steam that builds the pressure and maintains the heat inside the pressure cooker. The cover over the pan holding the food maintains the dry environment inside.

Braising

Braising usually starts by browning a less expensive cut of meat in a pan on top of the stove and then covering the meat with a small amount of liquid, adding a lid or covering to the pan, and slowly cooking it. Braising can take place on the stovetop, in the oven, or in a slow cooker or pressure cooker. The slow-cooking process tenderizes the meat. The cooking environment in the pressure cooker greatly reduces the braising time needed. For example, a roast that would normally take two and a half to three hours in the oven or on the stove only requires forty-five to sixty minutes in the pressure cooker.

Deglazing

The term refers to the process of ridding a pan of any remaining fat by putting it over a medium-high heat and then adding enough cooking liquid to let you scrape up any browned bits stuck to the bottom of the pan. Doing this step before you add the other ingredients for your sauce or gravy gives the end result more flavor and color.

Poaching

This is accomplished by gently simmering ingredients in broth, juice, water, wine, or other flavorful liquids until they're cooked through and tender.

Roasting

Roasting, like baking, is usually done in the oven, but generally at a higher oven temperature. Roasting meat in the moist environment inside a pressure cooker requires some trial and error because you can't rely on a programmable meat thermometer to tell you when the meat has reached the desired internal temperature. The upside is that the meat will roast much quicker when browned and then placed on the rack in a pressure cooker, and, even if it's cooked beyond your preferred preference, the meat will still be more moist than it would be if you had cooked it to that point in the dry environment of an oven.

Sautéing

This is the method of quickly cooking small or thin pieces of food in some oil or butter that has been brought to temperature in a sauté pan (or in the pressure cooker) over medium to medium-high heat.

DEALING WITH FOAM

If liquid or foam is released from the vent, remove the pressure cooker from the heat and wait until the pressure is released naturally. This problem can occur when the pressure cooker is filled beyond capacity; in this case, remove some of the ingredients before proceeding. Another possibility is that you're cooking a food that foams. Adding additional oil and cleaning the area around the pressure regulator should alleviate the problem.

Steaming

Steaming is the cooking method that uses the steam from the cooking liquid to cook the food.

Stewing

Like braising, stewing involves slowly cooking the food in a liquid; however, stewing involves a larger liquid-to-food ratio. In other words, you use far more liquid when you're stewing food. Not surprisingly, this method is most often used to make stew.

Stir-frying

This is a cooking process similar to sautéing that's used to cook larger, bite-sized pieces of meat or vegetables in oil.

Tempering

Tempering is the act of gradually increasing the temperature of one cooking ingredient by adding small amounts of a hotter ingredient to the first. For example, tempering beaten eggs by whisking small amounts of hot liquid into them before you add the eggs to the cooking pan lets them be mixed into the dish; tempering prevents them from scrambling instead.

Pressure Cooker Tips and Tricks

There will be a learning curve with each pressure cooker that you use. You also need to keep in mind that the same pressure cooker will behave differently on different stovetops. For example, electric burners usually retain heat longer than do gas burners; therefore, if you need to reduce the pressure when cooking over an electric burner, after you adjust the burner setting, you may need to lift the cooker off of the heat.

Also, as mentioned earlier in this chapter, pressure cookers are like any other pan in your kitchen: There's less chance that foods will burn or stick to the bottom of better pans with thicker pan bottoms. If burning is a problem with your pressure cooker, you can try one of these solutions:

* Add more liquid the next time you make that recipe.
* Begin to heat or bring liquids to a boil before you lock on the lid.
* Bring the cooker up to pressure over a lower heat.
* Use a heat diffuser.

There will be times when the pressure cooker will come to pressure almost immediately and other times when it can take twenty minutes or more to do so. Keep in mind that it can delay the time it takes the cooker to reach the desired pressure when you are cooking a much higher ratio of food to liquid or if the food was very cold when you began the cooking process.

After you've worked with your pressure cooker, you'll come to recognize the signs that the cooker is about to reach pressure by the sounds it makes. (The cooker will usually release some steam before the pressure gasket finally settles into place.) If the pressure cooker fails to come to pressure, chances are:

* The gasket isn't allowing for a tight seal. Coating the gasket in vegetable oil will sometimes help solve this problem. If it doesn't, you'll need to replace the gasket.
* The lid isn't properly locked into place.
* Something is clogging the pressure regulator. You'll need to use the quick release method so you can remove the lid and then follow the manufacturer's direction for cleaning the gasket before you can proceed.
* There isn't sufficient liquid in the cooker. If you believe this to be the case, you'll need to test the pressure by using the quick release method so that you can remove the lid, then add more liquid, lock the lid back into place, and try again.
* You have too much food in the pressure cooker. You'll need to remove some of the food and try again.

Tips for Using This Cookbook

Don't be afraid to experiment a little with the recipes in this cookbook. Swap your favorite ingredients for those you're not too fond of. Adjust cooking times and measurements to suit your preferences. Keep in mind that the browning and sautéing times given in the recipes are suggestions. Once you become familiar with your pressure cooker's quirks, you'll be able to gauge the correct burner temperature and the amount of time you will need to sauté or brown foods on your own.

As you prepare the dishes in this cookbook, make notes in the margins about which ones you, your family, and your friends preferred. Don't rely on your memory: If you think a recipe would benefit by adding a bit more seasoning, then note that too. Making such notes now will mean that someday, when you're ready to write out recipe cards, you'll be able to have an entire pressure cooker section in the recipe box.

As you get more comfortable with your pressure cooker, you can try adapting conventional recipes to use with the pressure cooker. Just remember to add the nonliquid ingredients first. For example, for a stew you'd add the meat and vegetables first and only add as much of the liquid called for in the recipe to cover the food and bring the liquid level up to the fill line. You can stir in more liquid later. Choose your cooking time based on what's required to cook the meat.

CHAPTER 2

Breakfasts and Brunches

Hash Browns with Smoked Sausage & Apples

Serves 4

2 tablespoons olive oil

2 tablespoons butter

1 (12-ounce) bag frozen hash brown potatoes

Salt and freshly ground black pepper, to taste

6 ounces cooked smoked sausage, coarsely chopped

2 medium apples, such as Golden Delicious, cut into thin slices

Optional: 1 teaspoon cinnamon; 1–2 tablespoons toasted walnuts, chopped; 1–2 tablespoons maple syrup

1. Add the oil and butter to the pressure cooker and bring to temperature over medium heat. Add the hash brown potatoes; sauté for 5 minutes, stirring occasionally, until they are thawed and just beginning to brown. Season with the salt and pepper.

2. Add the sausage and apple over the top of the potatoes. Sprinkle the cinnamon over the apples, top with the toasted walnuts, and drizzle with the maple syrup if using.

3. Lock the lid in place and bring to low pressure; maintain pressure for 6 minutes. Remove from the heat and quick-release the pressure. Serve.

Garden Tofu Scramble

Serves 2–4

16 ounces firm tofu, drained

1 teaspoon fresh lemon juice

1 teaspoon salt

1/2 teaspoon black pepper

1/2 teaspoon turmeric

1 tablespoon olive oil

1/2 cup broccoli florets, blanched

1/2 cup sliced button mushrooms

1/2 cup diced tomato

1 clove garlic, peeled and minced

1/4 cup water

2 tablespoons chopped parsley

1. In a large bowl, mash the tofu with your hands or a fork, then stir in the lemon juice, salt, pepper, and turmeric.

2. Bring the olive oil to medium heat in the pressure cooker. Add the broccoli and mushrooms and sauté for 5 minutes. Add the tomato and garlic, and sauté for an additional 30 seconds.

3. Pour in the tofu mixture and water, stir, then lock the lid into place. Bring to medium pressure and maintain for 6 minutes. Remove from the heat and allow pressure to release naturally. Remove the lid and stir in the parsley before serving.

Sausage & Cheese Scramble

Serves 8

1 tablespoon olive oil or vegetable oil

1 large sweet onion, peeled and diced

1 green bell pepper, seeded and diced

1 red bell pepper, seeded and diced

1 yellow or orange bell pepper, seeded and diced

1 pound ground sausage

1 (1-pound) bag frozen hash brown potatoes, thawed

8 large eggs

1/4 cup water or heavy cream

Optional: A few drops hot sauce

Salt and freshly ground black pepper, to taste

1/2 pound Cheddar cheese, grated

1. Add the oil to the pressure cooker and bring it to temperature over medium-high heat.

2. Add the onion and diced bell peppers; sauté until the onion is transparent, about 5 minutes. Stir in the sausage and hash brown potatoes.

3. Bring to low pressure; maintain for 10 minutes. Remove from the heat and quick-release the pressure. Remove the lid. Drain and discard any excess fat.

4. Return the pan to medium heat. Whisk together the eggs, water or heavy cream, hot sauce (if using), and salt and pepper.

5. Pour the eggs over the sausage-potato mixture. Stir to combine and scramble the eggs until they begin to set.

6. Add the cheese and continue to scramble until the eggs finish cooking and the cheese melts.

7. If you prefer, instead of stirring the cheese into the mixture, you can top it with the cheese, then cover the pressure cooker and continue to cook for 1–2 minutes or until the cheese is melted. Serve immediately.

Irish Oatmeal with Fruit

Serves 2

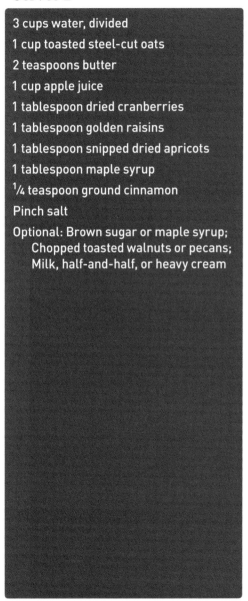

3 cups water, divided

1 cup toasted steel-cut oats

2 teaspoons butter

1 cup apple juice

1 tablespoon dried cranberries

1 tablespoon golden raisins

1 tablespoon snipped dried apricots

1 tablespoon maple syrup

¼ teaspoon ground cinnamon

Pinch salt

Optional: Brown sugar or maple syrup;
Chopped toasted walnuts or pecans;
Milk, half-and-half, or heavy cream

1. Place the rack in the pressure cooker; pour ½ cup of the water over the rack.

2. In a metal bowl that will fit inside the pressure cooker and rest on the rack, add the oats, butter, 2½ cups of the water, apple juice, cranberries, raisins, apricots, maple syrup, cinnamon, and salt; stir to combine.

3. Lock the lid into place. Bring to low pressure. For chewy oatmeal, maintain the pressure for 5 minutes. For creamy oatmeal, maintain pressure for 8 minutes.

4. Remove from the heat and allow pressure to release naturally. Use tongs to lift the metal bowl out of the pressure cooker.

5. Spoon the cooked oats into bowls. Serve warm, topped with brown sugar or additional maple syrup, chopped nuts, and milk, half-and-half, or heavy cream.

Irish Oatmeal with Fruit

Sausage Brunch Gravy

Serves 8

1 pound ground pork sausage

1 small sweet onion, peeled and diced

1 green bell pepper, seeded and diced

1 red bell pepper, seeded and diced

2 tablespoons butter

¼ cup all-purpose flour

2 cups half-and-half

Salt and freshly ground black pepper, to taste

1. Add the sausage, onion, and diced bell peppers to the pressure cooker. Fry over medium-high heat and break sausage apart for 5 minutes or until it begins to brown.

2. Lock the lid into place and bring to low pressure; maintain for 10 minutes. Remove from the heat and quick-release the pressure. Remove the lid. Drain and discard any excess fat.

3. Return the pressure cooker to medium-high heat. Add the butter and stir into the sausage mixture until it's melted.

4. Add the flour and stir-fry it into the meat for 1 minute, stirring continuously. Whisk in the half-and-half a little at a time.

5. Bring to a boil and then immediately reduce the heat; maintain a simmer for 3 minutes or until the gravy thickens. Taste for seasoning and add salt and pepper if needed.

Country Ham with Red-Eye Gravy

Serves 4

1 tablespoon lard or vegetable oil

4 (4-ounce) slices of country ham

¾ cup coffee

1 teaspoon sugar

1. Heat the lard or oil in the pressure cooker. Add ham and fry on both sides for 2 minutes. Add coffee. Lock the lid into place, bring to low pressure, and maintain for 8 minutes.

2. Remove from heat and quick-release the pressure. Remove ham to a serving platter. Add the sugar to the pan and stir until it dissolves, scraping the bottom of the pan as you do so. Pour over the ham and serve immediately.

Sausage Links Brunch

Serves 4

1 pound pork sausage links

4 large potatoes, peeled and sliced thin

1 medium sweet onion, peeled and diced

1 (16-ounce) can creamed corn

¼ teaspoon black pepper

¾ cup tomato juice

Salt, to taste

1. Add the sausage links to the pressure cooker and brown them over medium heat. Remove the sausages to a plate.

2. Layer the potatoes, onion, and corn in the cooker. Sprinkle on the pepper. Place sausage links on top of the corn.

3. Pour the tomato juice over the top of the other ingredients in the cooker. Lock the lid, bring to high pressure, and maintain for 7 minutes.

4. Remove from the heat and let sit for 10 minutes or until the pot returns to normal pressure. Taste for seasoning and add salt and additional pepper if needed.

Breakfast Hash

Serves 4

8 ounces ground sausage

$1/3$ cup water

1 (1-pound) bag frozen country-style hash brown potatoes, thawed

4 large eggs

1 cup grated Cheddar cheese

Optional: Salsa; $1/4$ cup minced fresh cilantro

1. Add the sausage to the pressure cooker; fry it over medium heat until it's browned and cooked through, breaking it apart as you do so.

2. Drain and discard any rendered fat. Pour in the water, stirring it into the meat, scraping up any meat stuck to the bottom of the pan.

3. Stir in the hash brown potatoes. Lightly beat the eggs and evenly pour them over the sausage and hash browns mixture.

4. Lock the lid into place and bring to low pressure; maintain pressure for 4 minutes.

5. Remove from the heat and quick-release the pressure. Remove the lid, evenly sprinkle the cheese over the top of the hash, and cover the pressure cooker.

6. Let sit for 5 minutes to allow the cheese to melt. Serve warm. Top each serving with salsa and fresh cilantro if desired.

Banana Nut Bread Oatmeal

Serves 2

³/4 cup water
1 cup milk or soymilk
1 cup quick-cooking oats
2 bananas, sliced
2 tablespoons brown sugar
2 teaspoons cinnamon
2 tablespoons chopped walnuts

1. Place all of the ingredients in the pressure cooker.

2. Lock the lid into place. Bring to high pressure and maintain for 5 minutes. Remove from the heat and allow pressure to release naturally.

3. Remove the lid and stir the oatmeal, adding more milk if desired.

Maple-Pecan Oatmeal

Serves 2

3/4 cup water
1 cup milk or soymilk
1 cup quick-cooking oats
2 tablespoons maple syrup
2 tablespoons chopped pecans

1. Place all of the ingredients in the pressure cooker.

2. Lock the lid into place. Bring to high pressure and maintain for 5 minutes. Remove from the heat and allow pressure to release naturally.

3. Remove the lid and stir the oatmeal, adding more milk if desired.

Grits

Chapter 2: Breakfasts and Brunches

Grits

Serves 4

4 cups water

1 teaspoon salt

$\frac{1}{2}$ teaspoon black pepper

1 cup stone-ground grits

1 tablespoon butter, or vegan
  margarine, such as Earth Balance

1. Bring the water, salt, and pepper to a boil in the pressure cooker over high heat. Slowly stir in the grits.

2. Lock the lid into place. Bring to high pressure and maintain for 10 minutes. Remove from the heat and allow pressure to release naturally.

3. Remove the lid and stir in butter before serving.

Red Pepper Grits

Serves 4

4 cups Vegetable Stock (see recipe in
  Chapter 4)

1 teaspoon salt

$\frac{1}{4}$ teaspoon dried thyme

1 cup stone-ground grits

$\frac{1}{2}$ tablespoon dried red pepper flakes

1. Bring the stock, salt, and thyme to a boil in the pressure cooker over high heat. Slowly stir in the grits.

2. Lock the lid into place. Bring to high pressure and maintain for 10 minutes. Remove from the heat and allow pressure to release naturally.

3. Remove the lid and stir in the red pepper flakes before serving.

Three Pepper Vegan Frittata

Serves 4

2 tablespoons olive oil

1 cup peeled and diced red potatoes

½ cup diced onion

½ cup diced red bell pepper

½ cup diced green bell pepper

1 teaspoon minced jalapeño

1 clove garlic, peeled and minced

¼ cup chopped parsley

16 ounces firm tofu

½ cup unsweetened soymilk

4 teaspoons cornstarch

2 teaspoons nutritional yeast

1 teaspoon mustard

½ teaspoon turmeric

1 teaspoon salt

1. Preheat the oven to 400°F.

2. Bring the olive oil to medium heat in the pressure cooker. Add the potatoes, onion, peppers, garlic, and parsley, and sauté for 3 minutes. Lock the lid in place and bring to high pressure; maintain pressure for 6 minutes. Remove from the heat and quick-release the pressure.

3. Combine the tofu, soymilk, cornstarch, nutritional yeast, mustard, turmeric, and salt in a blender or food processor until smooth, then pour the tofu mixture into the cooked potato mixture.

4. Spoon the mixture into an oiled quiche or pie pan. Bake for 45 minutes, or until the frittata is firm, then remove from heat and let stand before serving.

Spinach & Portobello Benedict

Serves 2

½ cup silken tofu
1 tablespoon lemon juice
1 teaspoon Dijon mustard
⅛ teaspoon cayenne pepper
⅛ teaspoon turmeric
1 tablespoon vegetable oil
Salt, to taste
1 tablespoon olive oil
4 small portobello mushroom caps
2 cups fresh spinach
2 English muffins, toasted

1. Add the silken tofu to a food processor and purée until smooth. Add the lemon juice, mustard, cayenne, and turmeric. Blend until well combined. With the food processor still running, slowly add the vegetable oil and blend until combined. Season with salt, to taste, to complete the vegan hollandaise sauce.

2. Pour the hollandaise into a small saucepan over low heat and cook until the sauce is warm. Keep warm until ready to serve.

3. Heat the olive oil in the pressure cooker over low heat. Add the mushroom caps and spinach and stir until coated with the oil.

4. Lock the lid into place. Bring to medium pressure and maintain for 3 minutes. Remove from the heat and quick-release the pressure.

5. Place two open-faced English muffins on each plate and top each half with one portobello cap and sautéed spinach. Drizzle with a spoonful of the warm vegan hollandaise to finish.

Home Fries

Serves 4

2 tablespoons olive oil

4 cups diced red potatoes

1½ teaspoons paprika

1 teaspoon chili powder

1½ teaspoons salt

1 teaspoon black pepper

1. Bring the olive oil to medium heat in the pressure cooker. Add the potatoes and sauté for about 3 minutes.

2. Add all remaining ingredients and stir. Lock the lid in place and bring to high pressure; maintain pressure for 7 minutes. Remove from the heat and quick-release the pressure.

Hash Browns

Serves 4

4 cups peeled and grated russet potatoes

2 tablespoons olive oil

2 tablespoons butter, or vegan margarine, such as Earth Balance

Salt and freshly ground black pepper, to taste

1. Prepare the potatoes and set aside.

2. Add the oil and butter to the pressure cooker and bring to temperature over medium heat.

3. Add the grated potatoes; sauté for 5 minutes, stirring occasionally, until they are just beginning to brown. Season with the salt and pepper. Use a wide metal spatula to press the potatoes down firmly in the pan.

4. Lock the lid in place and bring to low pressure; maintain pressure for 6 minutes. Remove from the heat and quick-release the pressure.

Home Fries

Tofu Ranchero

Serves 4

16 ounces firm tofu, drained

1 teaspoon fresh lemon juice

1 teaspoon salt

1/2 teaspoon black pepper

1/2 teaspoon turmeric

2 tablespoons olive oil, divided

1/4 cup diced onion

1 clove garlic, peeled and minced

8 corn tortillas

1 cup vegetarian refried beans, warmed

1/2 cup shredded cheese or vegan cheese

1/2 cup chipotle salsa

1. Preheat the oven to 350°F. In a large bowl, mash the tofu with your hands or a fork, then stir in the lemon juice, salt, pepper, and turmeric.

2. Bring 1 tablespoon olive oil to medium heat in the pressure cooker. Add the onion and sauté for 3 minutes. Add the garlic and sauté for an additional 30 seconds.

3. Pour in the tofu mixture, stir, then lock the lid into place. Bring to medium pressure and maintain for 6 minutes. Remove from the heat and allow pressure to release naturally.

4. Heat 1 tablespoon olive oil in a small sauté pan over medium heat. Cook the tortillas one at a time, until they begin to brown on each side.

5. Place all eight of the tortillas on one or two baking sheets. Divide the refried beans evenly among the tortillas, then top with the cooked tofu mixture. Sprinkle cheese over each of the tortillas, then bake until the cheese begins to melt.

6. Remove from the oven and top with salsa before serving.

Breakfast Burrito

Serves 4

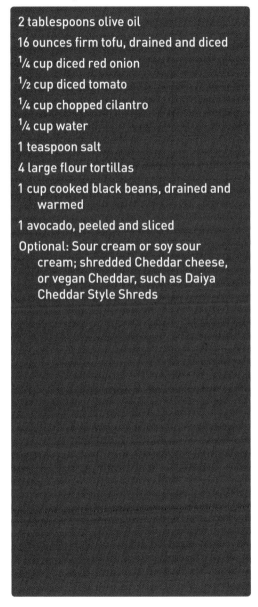

2 tablespoons olive oil

16 ounces firm tofu, drained and diced

¼ cup diced red onion

½ cup diced tomato

¼ cup chopped cilantro

¼ cup water

1 teaspoon salt

4 large flour tortillas

1 cup cooked black beans, drained and warmed

1 avocado, peeled and sliced

Optional: Sour cream or soy sour cream; shredded Cheddar cheese, or vegan Cheddar, such as Daiya Cheddar Style Shreds

1. Heat the olive oil in the pressure cooker over medium-high heat. Add the tofu, stir until well coated, and sauté until it begins to brown, about 5 minutes. Add the onion, tomato, cilantro, water, and salt.

2. Lock the lid into place. Bring to high pressure and maintain for 6 minutes. Remove from the heat and quick-release the pressure.

3. Steam or microwave the tortillas until softened, then lay one tortilla on a flat surface to build the burrito. Place ¼ of the tofu mixture, ¼ of the drained beans, and ¼ of the avocado slices in a line in the center of the tortilla.

4. Roll your burrito by first folding the sides of the tortilla over the filling. Then, while still holding the sides closed, fold the bottom of the tortilla over the filling. Next, roll the burrito from the bottom up, while still holding the sides closed and pushing the filling down into the burrito if it tries to spill out. Repeat for remaining burritos.

5. Top with sour cream and/or cheese, if desired.

Yeasty Tofu & Veggies

Serves 4

1 (16-ounce) package extra-firm tofu

2 tablespoons vegetable oil, divided

2 tablespoons soy sauce, divided

1 cup water

½ onion, peeled and diced

1 cup chopped broccoli, blanched

½ green bell pepper, seeded and chopped

½ zucchini, chopped

½ cup chopped yellow squash

¼ cup nutritional yeast

1. Wrap the block of tofu in paper towels and press for 5 minutes by adding weight on top. Remove the paper towels and cut the tofu into ½"-thick pieces. Add 1 tablespoon of oil to the pressure cooker and sauté the tofu until it is light brown on all sides. Add 1 tablespoon of soy sauce and sauté for 10 seconds more. Remove the tofu.

2. Place the water in the pressure cooker along with the steamer tray. Place the tofu on top of the steamer tray. Lock the lid into place; bring to high pressure and maintain for 5 minutes. Remove from the heat and allow pressure to release naturally.

3. Add 1 tablespoon of oil to a large pan and sauté the onions, broccoli, bell pepper, zucchini, and squash until tender. Add the tofu and 1 tablespoon soy sauce and sauté for 1 minute more. Sprinkle the nutritional yeast on top and serve.

CHAPTER 3

Appetizers and Bites

Hummus

Yield: About 2 cups

1 cup chickpeas

2 teaspoons vegetable oil

4 cups water

1 teaspoon dried parsley

1 clove garlic, peeled and minced

2 tablespoons tahini

Salt, to taste

2 tablespoons lemon juice

¼ cup extra-virgin olive oil or sesame oil

Optional: 6 tablespoons water or cooking liquid

1. Add the chickpeas, vegetable oil, and 4 cups of water to the pressure cooker. Lock the lid into place; bring to high pressure and maintain for 40 minutes. Remove from the heat and allow pressure to release naturally. Remove the lid and check that the beans are soft and cooked through. Drain the beans if they're cooked through; if not, lock the lid back into place and cook the beans on high pressure for another 5–10 minutes.

2. Add the drained, cooked beans, parsley, garlic, tahini, salt, and lemon juice to a food processor or blender. Pulse to combine. Remove the lid and scrape down the sides of the food processor or blender bowl.

3. Reattach the lid to the food processor or blender, and add the olive oil with the machine running. Process until smooth, adding water or reserved cooking liquid a tablespoon at a time if necessary.

Dhal

Yield: 2 cups

1 tablespoon olive oil

1 teaspoon unsalted butter

1 small onion, peeled and diced

2 teaspoons grated fresh ginger

1 serrano chili pepper, seeded and
    finely diced

1 clove garlic, peeled and minced

1/2 teaspoon garam masala

1/4 teaspoon ground turmeric

1/2 teaspoon dry mustard

1 cup dried yellow split peas

2 cups water

1/4 cup plain yogurt or sour cream

2 tablespoons minced fresh cilantro

1. Add the oil and butter to the pressure cooker and bring to temperature over medium heat. Add the onion, ginger, and chili; sauté for 3 minutes or until soft. Add the garlic, garam masala, turmeric, and dry mustard; sauté for an additional minute. Stir in the split peas. Pour in the water.

2. Lock on the lid. Bring the pressure cooker to high pressure; maintain for 8 minutes. Remove from the heat and allow pressure to release naturally. Transfer the cooked split pea mixture to a bowl; stir until cooled.

3. Add the yogurt or sour cream; whisk until smooth. Stir in the cilantro.

Cipolline Agrodolce (Sweet & Sour Pearl Onions)

Serves 6

1 pound cipolline (pearl onions), outer
    layer removed
½ cup water
⅛ teaspoon salt
1 bay leaf
4 tablespoons balsamic vinegar
1 tablespoon honey
1 tablespoon flour

1. Place the onions in the pressure cooker with the water, salt, and bay leaf. Close and lock the lid.

2. Turn the heat up to high. When the cooker reaches pressure, lower to the minimum heat needed to maintain pressure. Cook for 5–6 minutes at low pressure (3 minutes at high pressure).

3. While the onions are cooking, combine the balsamic vinegar, honey, and flour in a small saucepan. Stir over low heat until well combined (about 30 seconds).

4. When time is up for the onions, open the pressure cooker by releasing pressure.

5. Pour the balsamic vinegar mixture over the onions and mix well.

6. Transfer to a serving dish and serve hot, or let sit overnight in refrigerator prior to serving.

South of the Border Chicken Dip

Serves 24

3 slices bacon, diced

2 tablespoons olive oil

1 medium white onion, peeled and diced

3 cloves garlic, peeled and minced

½ cup minced fresh cilantro

⅓ cup salsa

¼ cup ketchup

½ cup chicken broth

1 teaspoon chili powder

1 pound chicken breast tenders, finely diced

Optional: 1 tablespoon all-purpose flour

1 cup (4 ounces) grated Monterey jack cheese

½ cup sour cream

Salt and freshly ground black pepper, to taste

Baked corn or flour tortilla chips

1. Add the bacon and oil to the pressure cooker; bring to temperature over medium heat and add the onion, garlic, and cilantro. Sauté for 3 minutes or until the onion is soft. Stir in the salsa, ketchup, broth, chili powder, and diced chicken. Lock the lid into place and bring to low pressure; maintain pressure for 6 minutes.

2. Remove the lid and simmer over medium heat to thicken the sauce. If needed, whisk the flour into the dip, bring to a boil, and then simmer for 2 minutes or until the flour taste is cooked out. Lower the heat and add the cheese, stirring constantly until it is melted into the dip. Fold in the sour cream. Taste for seasoning and add salt and pepper if desired. Serve warm with baked corn or flour tortilla chips.

Steamed Pears

Steamed Pears

Serves 4

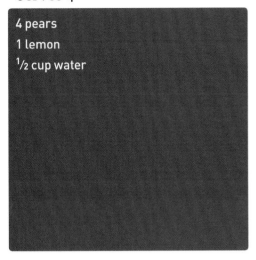

4 pears
1 lemon
½ cup water

1. Rinse and dry the pears. Halve them lengthwise. Use a melon baller to remove the core from each half. Cut the lemon in half and rub the cut end of the lemon over the cut ends of the pears or brush the pear halves with fresh lemon juice.

2. Add the water to the pressure cooker. Place the rack in the pressure cooker and place a heatproof plate onto the rack. Arrange the pears on the plate. Lock the lid into place and bring to high pressure; maintain pressure for 4 minutes. Remove the pressure cooker from the heat, quick-release the pressure, and remove the lid. Use a slotted spoon to carefully transfer the pears to a serving plate. Serve warm or allow to cool slightly and then cover the plate and refrigerate until needed.

Baba Ghanoush

Yield: 1½ cups

1 tablespoon olive or sesame oil
1 large eggplant, peeled and diced
4 cloves garlic, peeled and minced
½ cup water
3 tablespoons fresh parsley
½ teaspoon salt
2 tablespoons fresh lemon juice
2 tablespoons tahini
1 tablespoon extra-virgin olive oil

1. Add the olive or sesame oil to the pressure cooker and bring to temperature over medium heat. Peel and dice the eggplant and add it to the pressure cooker. Sauté the eggplant in the oil until it begins to get soft. Add the garlic and sauté for 30 seconds. Add the water.

2. Lock on the lid. Bring to high pressure; maintain pressure for 4 minutes. Remove the pan from the heat, quick-release the pressure, and remove the lid.

3. Strain the cooked eggplant and garlic and add to a food processor or blender along with the parsley, salt, lemon juice, and tahini. Pulse to process. Add the extra-virgin olive oil and process until smooth.

Asparagus with Yogurt Crème

Serves 4

2 cups plain whole yogurt

1 cup water

1 pound asparagus, trimmed

1¼ teaspoons salt

1. To make the yogurt crème, put the yogurt in a fine mesh strainer over a bowl and refrigerate for about 4 hours, or until the yogurt in the strainer has reached the consistency of sour cream.

2. Place water in the pressure cooker and add the steamer basket.

3. Lay asparagus flat in steamer basket. If it does not fit in one layer, make a second layer perpendicular to the first. Sprinkle with salt. Close and lock the lid.

4. Turn the heat up to high. When the cooker reaches pressure, lower to the minimum heat needed to maintain pressure. Cook for 2–3 minutes at high pressure.

5. When time is up, open the pressure cooker by quick-releasing the pressure.

6. Serve with yogurt crème.

Lemon & Rosemary Cannellini Cream

Serves 6

2 tablespoons vegetable oil

1 scallion, chopped

1½ cups dried cannellini beans, rinsed

3 cups water

Juice and zest of 1 lemon

½ teaspoon white pepper

2 sprigs rosemary (1 sprig finely chopped and 1 whole sprig)

1 tablespoon extra-virgin olive oil

1. Heat vegetable oil in an uncovered pressure cooker over medium heat. Add the scallion and sauté until softened (about 3 minutes). Add cannellini beans and water. Close and lock the lid.

2. Turn the heat up to high. When the cooker reaches pressure, lower to the minimum heat needed to maintain pressure. Cook 25–30 minutes at high pressure.

3. Open with the natural release method—move the pressure cooker to a cool burner and wait for the pressure to come down on its own (about 10 minutes). For electric pressure cookers, disengage the "keep warm" mode or unplug the cooker and open when the pressure indicator has gone down (20–30 minutes).

4. Drain the beans, let them cool, and pour them into a food processor. Add lemon juice, lemon zest, pepper, chopped rosemary, and olive oil. Purée until smooth.

5. Pour into a serving dish and garnish with fresh rosemary sprig.

Steamed Artichokes

Serves 6

6 artichokes
1 cup water
Juice of 1 lemon

1. Clean the artichokes by cutting off the top ⅓ and removing the tough exterior leaves.

2. Place artichokes upright in the steamer basket. Fill the pressure cooker base with water and lemon juice, and then lower the steamer basket into the cooker. Close and lock the lid.

3. The cooking time will depend on the size of the artichokes. A large globe artichoke that almost fills the pressure cooker could take 10 minutes, while medium artichokes only need about 5 minutes.

4. Turn the heat up to high. When the cooker reaches pressure, lower to the minimum heat needed to maintain pressure. Cook 5–10 minutes at high pressure.

5. When time is up, open the pressure cooker by quick-releasing the pressure.

6. Lift the artichokes very carefully out of the pressure cooker (they will be so tender, they may fall apart) and serve.

Steamed Spring Rolls

Serves 12

1 cup shredded cabbage

1 cup sliced bamboo shoots

¼ cup chopped cilantro

2 cloves garlic, peeled and minced

5 shiitake mushrooms, sliced

2 carrots, grated

1 teaspoon soy sauce

1 teaspoon rice wine vinegar

12 spring roll wrappers

2 cups water, divided

1. Combine the cabbage, bamboo shoots, cilantro, garlic, mushrooms, carrots, soy sauce, and rice wine vinegar in a medium bowl. Stir until just combined.

2. Soak the spring roll wrappers in ½ cup water and place them on a flat surface.

3. Top each wrapper with an equal amount of the cabbage mixture, making a row down the center. Roll up the wrappers, tuck in the ends, and place side by side in the pressure cooker steamer basket.

4. Add 1½ cups water to the pressure cooker and lower in the steamer basket. Close and lock the lid.

5. Turn the heat up to high. When the cooker reaches pressure, lower to the minimum heat needed to maintain pressure. Cook for 3–4 minutes at high pressure.

6. When time is up, open the pressure cooker by quick-releasing the pressure. Remove rolls immediately and place on a serving platter.

Mini Cabbage Rolls

Yield: 30 rolls

1 medium head savoy cabbage

3 cups water, divided

1 pound lean ground beef

1 cup long-grain rice

1 red bell pepper, seeded and minced

1 medium onion, peeled and diced

1 cup Vegetable Stock (see recipe in Chapter 4)

1 tablespoon extra-virgin olive oil

2 tablespoons minced, fresh mint

1 teaspoon dried tarragon

1 teaspoon salt

1/2 teaspoon freshly ground black pepper

2 tablespoons lemon juice

1. Wash the cabbage. Remove the large, outer leaves and set aside. Remove the remaining cabbage leaves and place them in the pressure cooker. Pour in 1 cup water and lock on the lid. Bring to low pressure; maintain the pressure for 1 minute. Quick-release the pressure. Drain the cabbage leaves in a colander and then move them to a cotton towel.

2. In a mixing bowl, add the ground beef, rice, bell pepper, onion, stock, extra-virgin olive oil, mint, tarragon, salt, and pepper. Stir to combine.

3. Place the reserved (uncooked) cabbage leaves on the bottom of the pressure cooker to keep the rolls from getting scorched.

4. Remove the stem running down the center of each steamed cabbage leaf and tear each leaf in half lengthwise. Place 1 tablespoon of the ground beef mixture in the center of each cabbage piece. Loosely fold the sides of the leaf over the filling and then fold the top and bottom of the leaf over the folded sides. As you complete them, place each stuffed cabbage leaf in the pressure cooker.

5. Pour 2 cups water and the lemon juice over the stuffed cabbage rolls. Close and lock the lid.

6. Turn the heat up to high. When the cooker reaches pressure, lower to the minimum heat needed to maintain pressure. Cook 15–20 minutes at high pressure.

7. Open with the natural release method—move the pressure cooker to a cool burner and wait for the pressure to come down on its own (about 10 minutes). For electric pressure cookers, disengage the "keep warm" mode or unplug the cooker and open when the pressure indicator has gone down (20–30 minutes).

8. Carefully move the stuffed cabbage rolls to a serving platter by piercing each one with a toothpick.

Spiced Peaches

Serves 6

2 (15-ounce) cans sliced peaches in syrup

$1/4$ cup water

1 tablespoon white wine vinegar

$1/8$ teaspoon ground allspice

1 cinnamon stick

4 whole cloves

$1/2$ teaspoon ground ginger

Pinch cayenne pepper

Optional: 1 tablespoon candied ginger, minced; 3 whole black peppercorns

1. Add all of the ingredients to the pressure cooker. Stir to mix. Lock the lid into place and bring to low pressure; maintain pressure for 3 minutes. Remove the pressure cooker from the heat, quick-release the pressure, and remove the lid.

2. Remove and discard the cinnamon stick, cloves, and peppercorns if used.

3. Return the pressure cooker to medium heat. Simmer and stir for 5 minutes to thicken the syrup.

4. Serve warm or chilled. To store, allow to cool and then refrigerate for up to a week.

Stuffed Grape Leaves

Serves 16

⅓ cup olive oil

4 scallions, minced

⅓ cup minced fresh mint

⅓ cup minced fresh parsley

3 cloves garlic, peeled and minced

1 cup long-grain white rice

2 cups vegetable broth

1 teaspoon salt

¼ teaspoon freshly ground black pepper

½ teaspoon grated lemon zest

1 (16-ounce) jar grape leaves

2 cups water

½ cup fresh lemon juice

1. Bring the oil to temperature in the pressure cooker over medium-high heat. Add the scallions, mint, and parsley; sauté for 2 minutes or until the scallions are soft. Add the garlic and sauté for an additional 30 seconds. Add the rice and stir-fry in the sautéed vegetables and herbs for 1 minute. Add the broth, salt, pepper, and lemon zest; stir to mix. Lock the lid into place. Bring to high pressure; maintain pressure for 8 minutes.

2. Quick-release the pressure. Remove lid and transfer the rice mixture to a bowl.

3. Drain the grape leaves. Rinse them thoroughly in warm water and then arrange them rib side up on a work surface. Trim away any thick ribs. Spoon about 2 teaspoons of the rice mixture on each grape leaf; fold the sides of each leaf over the filling and then roll it from the bottom to the top. Repeat with each leaf. Pour the water into the pressure cooker. Place a steamer basket in the pressure cooker and arrange the stuffed grape leaves seam side down in the basket. Pour the lemon juice over the stuffed grape leaves and then press heavy plastic wrap down around them.

4. Lock the lid into place. Bring to high pressure; maintain pressure for 10 minutes.

5. Quick-release the pressure. Remove the lid. Lift the steamer basket out of the pressure cooker and, leaving the plastic in place, let the stuffed grape leaves rest for 5 minutes. Serve hot or cold.

Stuffed Grape Leaves

Chickpea-Parsley-Dill Dip

Yield: 2 cups

1 cup dried chickpeas

8 cups water, divided

3 tablespoons olive oil, divided

2 garlic cloves, peeled and minced

1/8 cup fresh parsley, chopped

1/8 cup fresh dill, chopped

1 tablespoon fresh lemon juice

2 tablespoons water

3/4 teaspoon salt

1. Add the chickpeas and 4 cups water to the pressure cooker. Lock the lid into place; bring to high pressure for 1 minute. Remove from the heat and quick-release the pressure.

2. Drain the water, rinse the chickpeas, and add to the pressure cooker again with the remaining 4 cups of water. Let soak for 1 hour.

3. Add 1 tablespoon olive oil. Lock the lid into place; bring to high pressure and maintain for 20 minutes. Remove from the heat and allow pressure to release naturally. Drain chickpeas and water.

4. Add the drained, cooked chickpeas, garlic, parsley, dill, lemon juice, and water to a food processor or blender. Blend for about 30 seconds.

5. With the lid still in place, slowly add the remaining oil while still blending, then add the salt.

Baked Potato Skins

Serves 6

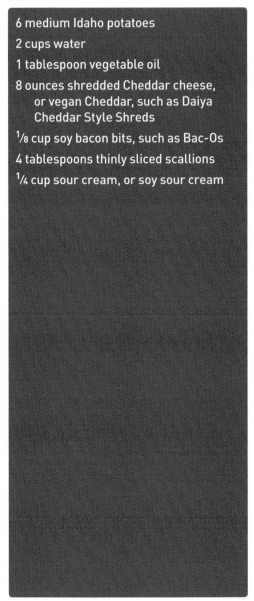

6 medium Idaho potatoes

2 cups water

1 tablespoon vegetable oil

8 ounces shredded Cheddar cheese, or vegan Cheddar, such as Daiya Cheddar Style Shreds

⅛ cup soy bacon bits, such as Bac-Os

4 tablespoons thinly sliced scallions

¼ cup sour cream, or soy sour cream

1. Preheat the oven to 400°F.

2. Wash the potatoes, then slice each in half lengthwise. Pour 2 cups water into the pressure cooker. Add the steamer basket and arrange the potatoes in one or two layers.

3. Lock the lid into place. Bring to high pressure; maintain pressure for 10 minutes. Quick-release the pressure, then remove the lid.

4. Remove the potatoes from the pressure cooker and scoop out the inside, leaving a ¼"-thick shell.

5. Brush the scooped out shell of each potato with oil and arrange on an ungreased baking sheet.

6. Cook the potato skins for 15 minutes, or until the edges begin to brown, then remove from the oven.

7. Fill the potato skins with the cheese and bake for an additional 5–10 minutes, or until the cheese has melted.

8. Top each skin with soy bacon bits, sliced scallions, and a dollop of sour cream.

Tomatillo Salsa

Serves 8

1 pound tomatillos, paper removed

Water, as needed

2 jalapeños, stemmed, seeded, and chopped

½ onion, peeled and chopped

½ cup cold water

½ cup chopped cilantro

2 teaspoons salt

1. Cut the tomatillos in half and then place in the pressure cooker. Add enough water to cover the tomatillos.

2. Lock the lid into place; bring to high pressure and maintain for 2 minutes. Remove from the heat and allow pressure to release naturally.

3. Add the drained, cooked tomatillos, jalapeños, onion, and cold water to a food processor or blender. Blend until well combined.

4. Add the cilantro and salt and pulse until combined. Chill the salsa before serving.

Boiled Peanuts

Serves 8

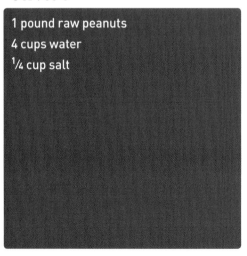

1 pound raw peanuts

4 cups water

¼ cup salt

1. Rinse the peanuts under cold water and then place in the pressure cooker. Add the water and salt. Close and lock the pressure cooker.

2. Turn the heat up to high. When the cooker reaches pressure, lower to the minimum heat needed to maintain pressure. Cook 20–40 minutes at high pressure.

3. When time is up, open the pressure cooker by quick-releasing the pressure.

4. Strain and enjoy!

CHAPTER 4

Stocks, Soups, and Chilis

Sun-Dried Tomato Soup

Serves 6

2½ tablespoons unsalted butter

1 stalk celery, finely diced

1 medium carrot, peeled and finely diced

1 small sweet onion, peeled and diced

1 teaspoon dried basil

½ teaspoon dried marjoram

2 tablespoons unbleached all-purpose flour

2 (15-ounce) cans diced tomatoes

4 whole sun-dried tomatoes

1 teaspoon sugar

⅛ teaspoon baking soda

2½ cups vegetable or chicken broth

Salt and freshly ground black pepper, to taste

1. Melt the butter in the pressure cooker over medium heat. Add the celery and carrot; sauté for 2 minutes. Stir in the onion, basil, and marjoram; sauté for 3 minutes or until the onion is soft. Add the flour; stir and cook for 2 minutes. Stir in the remaining ingredients.

2. Lock the lid into place. Bring to high pressure; maintain pressure for 8 minutes. Remove from the heat and quick-release the pressure. Remove the lid. Use an immersion blender to purée the soup. If you don't have an immersion blender, you can transfer the soup in batches to a blender or food processor, purée it, and then return it to the pot or a soup tureen. Taste for seasoning and add additional salt and pepper if needed.

Chapter 4: Stocks, Soups, and Chilis

Re-Fashioned Potato Soup

Serves 4

1 tablespoon extra-virgin olive oil

1 onion, peeled and diced

1 stalk celery, diced

4 medium potatoes, peeled and diced

6 cups Vegetable Stock (see recipe in this chapter)

2 teaspoons salt

½ teaspoon white pepper

1 cup whole plain yogurt

¼ cup chopped chives or parsley

1. Heat olive oil in an uncovered pressure cooker over medium heat. Sauté the onion and celery (about 5 minutes). Add potatoes and stock. Close and lock the lid.

2. Turn the heat up to high. When the cooker reaches pressure, lower the heat to the minimum needed to maintain pressure. Cook for 5–8 minutes at high pressure.

3. Open with the natural release method—move the pressure cooker to a cool burner and wait for the pressure to come down on its own (about 10 minutes). For electric pressure cookers, disengage the "keep warm" mode or unplug the cooker and open when the pressure indicator has gone down (20–30 minutes).

4. Purée with immersion blender, then add salt and white pepper. Stir in the yogurt and ladle into individual bowls. Garnish with chives or parsley.

Portuguese Kale Soup

Chapter 4: Stocks, Soups, and Chilis

Portuguese Kale Soup

Serves 6

1 pound kale

1 tablespoon extra-virgin olive oil

1 large yellow onion, peeled and thinly sliced

½ pound linguica or kielbasa, sliced

4 large potatoes, peeled and diced

4 cups chicken broth

2 (15-ounce) cans cannellini beans, rinsed and drained

Salt and freshly ground black pepper, to taste

1. Trim the large ribs from the kale. Slice it into thin strips. Put the kale strips into a bowl of cold water and soak for an hour; drain well.

2. Add the oil, onions, and linguica or kielbasa to the pressure cooker; stir to combine. Place over medium heat; sauté for 5 minutes or until the onions are soft. Add the potatoes, chicken broth, drained kale, and beans. Lock the lid into place and bring to low pressure; maintain pressure for 8 minutes. Remove from the heat and allow pressure to release naturally for 5 minutes. Quick-release any remaining pressure and remove the lid. Taste for seasoning and add salt and pepper to taste.

Split Pea Soup

Serves 6

4 strips bacon, diced

1 large sweet onion, peeled and diced

2 large potatoes, peeled and diced

2 large carrots, peeled and sliced

1 cup dried green split peas, rinsed

4 cups chicken broth

2 smoked ham hocks

Salt and freshly ground black pepper, to taste

1. Add bacon to the pressure cooker. Fry over medium heat until bacon begins to render its fat. Add onion; sauté for 3 minutes or until soft. Stir in diced potatoes; sauté for 3 minutes. Add carrots, split peas, broth, and ham hocks. Lock lid into place and bring to low pressure; maintain pressure for 15 minutes. Remove from the heat and allow pressure to release naturally.

2. Remove lid. Use a slotted spoon to remove ham hocks; allow to cool until the meat can be removed from the bones. Taste split peas. Remove from heat and quick-release pressure. Stir ham removed from the hocks into soup. Return soup to medium heat and bring to a simmer. Salt and pepper to taste.

Lentil & Black Bean Chili

Serves 4

1 tablespoon vegetable oil

1 red onion, peeled and diced

1 green bell pepper, seeded and chopped

1 yellow bell pepper, seeded and chopped

2 cloves garlic, peeled and smashed

½ teaspoon cumin

½ teaspoon hot pepper flakes

1 teaspoon oregano

1 cup dried lentils

1 cup black beans, soaked

2½ cups water

1 cup fresh or frozen corn

Zest and juice of 1 lime

Grated Cheddar cheese, for garnish

1. Add all of the ingredients, except for the corn and lime, to the pressure cooker. Close and lock the lid.

2. Turn the heat up to high. When the cooker reaches pressure, lower the heat to the minimum needed to maintain pressure. Cook for 8–10 minutes at high pressure.

3. Open with the natural release method—move the pressure cooker to a cool burner and wait for the pressure to come down on its own (about 10 minutes). For electric pressure cookers, disengage the "keep warm" mode or unplug the cooker. After 10 minutes, release the rest of the pressure using the valve.

4. Add the corn, stir well, then close the pressure cooker. Let sit (without turning it on again) to allow the residual heat of the pressure cooker to warm the corn for 5 minutes.

5. Stir in the lime juice and zest just before serving.

6. Ladle into individual bowls and serve with a dusting of cheese.

Thai Carrot Soup

Serves 8

1 tablespoon olive oil

1 onion, peeled and diced

2 cloves garlic, peeled and minced

3 teaspoons curry powder

1 bay leaf

1 pound carrots, peeled and roughly chopped

4 cups Vegetable Stock (see recipe in this chapter)

1 cup unsweetened coconut milk

1 teaspoon salt

½ teaspoon black pepper

¼ cup thinly sliced basil

1. Heat olive oil in an uncovered pressure cooker over medium heat. Sauté the onion until soft (about 5 minutes). Add the garlic and curry powder and sauté for an additional 30 seconds. Then, add the rest of the ingredients except for the basil. Close and lock the lid.

2. Turn the heat up to high. When the cooker reaches pressure, lower the heat to the minimum needed to maintain pressure. Cook for 5–7 minutes at high pressure.

3. Open with the natural release method—move the pressure cooker to a cool burner and wait for the pressure to come down on its own (about 10 minutes). For electric pressure cookers, disengage the "keep warm" mode or unplug the cooker. After 10 minutes, release the rest of the pressure using the valve.

4. Remove the bay leaf. Purée using an immersion blender. Garnish individual bowls with basil, and serve.

Fresh Tomato Soup

Serves 4

8 medium fresh tomatoes

¼ teaspoon sea salt

1 cup water

½ teaspoon baking soda

2 cups milk, half-and-half, or heavy cream

Freshly ground black pepper, to taste

1. Wash, peel, seed, and dice the tomatoes. Add them and any tomato juice you can retain to the pressure cooker. Stir in the salt and water. Lock the lid into place. Place the pressure cooker over medium heat and bring to low pressure; maintain pressure for 2 minutes. Quick-release the pressure and remove the lid.

2. Stir the baking soda into the tomato mixture. Once it's stopped bubbling and foaming, stir in your choice of milk, half-and-half, or cream. Cook and stir for several minutes or until the soup is brought to temperature. Taste for seasoning and add additional salt if needed, and pepper, to taste.

White Bean with Garlic & Kale Soup

Serves 8

2 cups dried cannellini beans

Water, as needed

2 tablespoons olive oil

½ cup thinly sliced onion

6 garlic cloves, peeled and thinly sliced

2 teaspoons dried oregano

1 (6-ounce) can tomato paste

2 tablespoons red wine vinegar

8 cups Vegetable Stock (see recipe in this chapter)

3 cups chopped kale

Salt and black pepper, to taste

1. Rinse the cannellini beans; soak for 8 hours in enough water to cover them by more than 1". Drain.

2. Bring the oil to temperature in the pressure cooker over medium heat. Add the onion and sauté until golden brown. Add the garlic and sauté for about 1 minute. Add the rest of the ingredients.

3. Lock the lid into place and bring to high pressure. Cook for about 10 minutes. Remove from the heat and allow pressure to release naturally. Taste for seasoning and add more salt and pepper if needed.

Fresh Tomato Soup

Cauliflower & Fennel Velouté

Serves 6

1 tablespoon olive oil

1 medium onion, peeled and chopped

½ fennel bulb, chopped (about the same quantity chopped as the onion)

1½ teaspoons salt

1 teaspoon white pepper

1 large head of cauliflower, cut into florets

1 bay leaf

5 cups Vegetable Stock (see recipe in this chapter)

2 tablespoons butter

¼ cup flour

1. Heat olive oil in an uncovered pressure cooker over medium heat. Add the onion, fennel, salt, and pepper, and sauté until the onion and fennel are softened, about 5 minutes. Add the cauliflower, bay leaf, and stock. Scrape the brown bits off the bottom of the pan and incorporate into the liquid. Close and lock the lid.

2. Turn the heat up to high. When the cooker reaches pressure, lower the heat to the minimum needed to maintain pressure. Cook for 5–7 minutes at high pressure.

3. Open the pressure cooker by quick-releasing the pressure.

4. Remove the bay leaf and add the butter and flour. Simmer for 3–5 minutes.

5. Before serving, use an immersion blender to purée the contents of the cooker.

Seafood Chowder

Serves 6

2 tablespoons butter

2 large leeks

4 cups fish broth or clam juice

2 cups water

6 medium russet or Idaho baking potatoes, peeled and diced

1 bay leaf

Salt and freshly ground black pepper, to taste

1 pound scrod or other firm white fish

½ teaspoon dried thyme

½ cup heavy cream

1. Melt the butter in the pressure cooker over medium heat. Cut off the root end of the leeks and discard any bruised outer leaves. Slice the leeks. Rinse in running water to remove any dirt; drain and dry. Add to the pressure cooker and sauté in the butter for 2 minutes. Stir in the broth, water, and potatoes. Add the bay leaf, salt, and pepper.

2. Lock the lid into place and bring to high pressure; maintain pressure for 4 minutes. Quick-release the pressure and remove the lid. Remove and discard the bay leaf.

3. Cut the fish into bite-sized pieces and add to the pressure cooker. Simmer for 3 minutes or until the fish is opaque and flakes easily. Stir in the thyme and cream.

4. Leave the pan on the heat, stirring occasionally, until the cream comes to temperature. Taste for seasoning; add additional salt and pepper if needed.

New England Clam Chowder

Serves 4

4 (6½-ounce) cans chopped clams

4 slices bacon

1 stalk celery, finely diced

2 large shallots, peeled and minced

1 pound red potatoes, peeled and diced

2½ cups unsalted chicken or vegetable broth

Optional: 1 tablespoon chopped fresh thyme

1 cup frozen corn, thawed

2 cups milk

1 cup heavy cream

Sea salt and freshly ground black pepper, to taste

1. Drain the clams. Reserve the liquid to add along with the broth. Set the clams aside.

2. Dice the bacon and add to the pressure cooker. Fry over medium-high heat until the bacon is crisp enough to crumble. Add the celery; sauté for 3 minutes.

3. Add the shallots; sauté for 3 minutes. Stir in the potatoes; stir-fry briefly in the bacon fat and vegetable mixture to coat the potatoes in the fat. Stir in the clam liquid, broth, and thyme if using.

4. Lock the lid into place and bring to high pressure; maintain pressure for 5 minutes. Lower the heat to warm and allow pressure to drop naturally for 10 minutes. Quick-release any remaining pressure and remove the lid.

5. Stir in the corn, milk, cream, and reserved clams. Bring to a simmer (but do not boil); simmer for 5 minutes or until everything is heated through. Taste for seasoning and add salt and pepper if needed.

Mushroom Beef Stew with Dumplings

Serves 8

1 tablespoon shortening or butter

1½ cups biscuit mix (e.g., Bisquick)

⅔ cup milk

1 large egg

1 (3-pound) English or chuck roast

2 (4-ounce) cans sliced mushrooms, drained

1 (10¾-ounce) can condensed cream of mushroom soup

1 (10½-ounce) can condensed French onion soup

1 tablespoon Worcestershire sauce

2 cups water

1 (24-ounce) bag frozen vegetables for stew, thawed

Salt and freshly ground black pepper, to taste

1. To make the dumpling batter, cut shortening or butter into biscuit mix until crumbly. Combine milk and beaten egg; add to dry mixture. Stir until just blended. Set aside. When you cook the dumplings in the stew, small drops of batter will suffice; they expand in the hot liquid.

2. Trim and discard any fat from the roast. Cut into bite-sized pieces and add meat, drained mushrooms, soups, Worcestershire sauce, and water to the pressure cooker.

3. Lock the lid into place and bring to low pressure; maintain pressure for 30 minutes. Quick-release the pressure and remove the lid.

4. Stir in the thawed frozen vegetables. Bring to a simmer and then drop tablespoon-sized dollops of the dumpling batter into the bubbling stew.

5. Lock the lid into place and bring to low pressure; maintain pressure for 5 minutes. Quick-release the pressure and remove the lid.

6. Stir the stew, being careful not to break the dumplings apart. (If dumplings aren't yet puffy and cooked through, loosely cover the pan and let the stew simmer for a few more minutes.) Taste for seasoning and add salt and pepper if needed.

Butternut Squash & Ginger Soup

Chapter 4: Stocks, Soups, and Chilis

Butternut Squash & Ginger Soup

Serves 6

1 tablespoon olive oil

1 large onion, peeled and roughly chopped

1 sprig sage

1 teaspoon salt

¼ teaspoon white pepper

4 pounds butternut squash, peeled, seeded, and cubed

1½" piece of fresh ginger, or 1 teaspoon dry ginger

¼ teaspoon nutmeg

4 cups Vegetable Stock (see recipe in this chapter)

½ cup toasted pumpkin seeds

1. Heat olive oil in an uncovered pressure cooker over medium heat. Sauté onions with the sage, salt, and pepper. When the onions are soft (approximately 5 minutes), push onions aside and add a handful of squash cubes to cover the bottom of pressure cooker.

2. Let the squash brown for about 10 minutes, stirring infrequently. Add the rest of the squash as well as the ginger, nutmeg, and stock. Close and lock the lid.

3. Turn the heat up to high. When the cooker reaches pressure, lower the heat to the minimum needed to maintain pressure. Cook for 10–15 minutes at high pressure.

4. When time is up, open the pressure cooker by quick-releasing the pressure.

5. Remove the piece of ginger (if used) and sage stem. Purée the contents of the pressure cooker with an immersion blender and serve garnished with pumpkin seeds.

Chicken in Beer Stew

Serves 6

1 teaspoon salt

½ tablespoon garlic powder

½ teaspoon cayenne pepper

2 tablespoons unbleached all-purpose flour

2 pounds boneless, skinless chicken thighs

2 tablespoons olive or vegetable oil

1 small green bell pepper, seeded and diced

1 small red bell pepper, seeded and diced

1 stalk celery, diced

1 medium onion, peeled and diced

1 jalapeño pepper, seeded and diced

2 cloves garlic, peeled and minced

1 bay leaf

1 teaspoon marjoram

1 (8-ounce) can tomato sauce

1 (12-ounce) bottle dark beer

½ cup chicken broth

2 teaspoons Worcestershire sauce

1 tablespoon bacon fat or lard

Freshly ground black pepper, to taste

1. Add the salt, garlic powder, cayenne pepper, and flour to a large zip-closure plastic bag; shake the bag to mix the spices into the flour.

2. Trim and discard any fat from the chicken thighs and cut them into bite-sized pieces.

3. Add the thigh pieces to the bag and shake to coat them in the seasoned flour.

4. Bring the oil to temperature in the pressure cooker over medium-high heat. Add the chicken in batches; stir-fry for 3–5 minutes or until browned. Reserve leftover seasoned flour.

5. Remove the browned chicken pieces and keep warm.

6. Reduce heat to medium. Add the green bell pepper, red bell pepper, and celery; sauté for 3 minutes.

7. Stir in the onion; sauté for 3 minutes or until the onion is soft. Add the jalapeño pepper and garlic; sauté for 30 seconds.

8. Stir in the bay leaf, marjoram, tomato sauce, beer, chicken broth, chicken pieces, and Worcestershire sauce.

9. Lock the lid into place and bring to low pressure; maintain pressure for 20 minutes. Quick-release the pressure and remove the lid. Remove and discard the bay leaf.

10. While the chicken mixture cooks under pressure, bring the bacon fat or lard to temperature in a cast-iron skillet over medium heat.

11. Whisk in the reserved seasoned flour and enough water to make a paste. Cook and stir constantly for about 10 minutes or until the roux turns the color of peanut butter.

12. Whisk some of the juices from the pressure cooker into the roux in the skillet to loosen the mixture, and then stir the roux into the mixture in the pressure cooker.

13. Bring the mixture to a simmer; simmer for 3 minutes or until thickened. Taste for seasoning; add additional salt and Worcestershire sauce, if needed, and black pepper to taste. Serve.

Corn Chowder

Serves 6

2 tablespoons butter

4 large leeks

4 cups chicken broth

2 cups water

6 medium russet or Idaho baking potatoes, peeled and diced

1 bay leaf

Salt and freshly ground black pepper, to taste

1½ cups fresh or frozen corn

½ teaspoon dried thyme

Pinch sugar

½ cup heavy cream

1. Melt the butter in the pressure cooker over medium heat. Cut off the root end of the leeks and discard any bruised outer leaves. Slice the leeks. Rinse in running water to remove any dirt; drain and dry. Add to the pressure cooker and sauté in the butter for 2 minutes. Stir in the broth, water, and potatoes. Add the bay leaf, salt, and pepper.

2. Lock the lid into place and bring to high pressure; maintain pressure for 4 minutes. Quick-release the pressure and remove the lid. Remove and discard the bay leaf.

3. Stir in the corn, thyme, sugar, and cream. Leave the pan on the heat, stirring occasionally, until the corn and cream come to temperature. Taste for seasoning; add additional salt and pepper if needed.

Corn Chowder

Chapter 4: Stocks, Soups, and Chilis

Vegetable Stock

Yield: 4 cups

2 large onions, peeled and halved

2 medium carrots, peeled and cut into large pieces

3 stalks celery, cut in half

10 peppercorns

1 bay leaf

4½ cups water

1. Add the onions, carrots, and celery to the pressure cooker. Add the peppercorns, bay leaf, and water to completely cover the vegetables. Close and lock the lid.

2. Turn the heat up to high. When the cooker reaches pressure, lower the heat to the minimum needed to maintain pressure. Cook for 10–15 minutes at high pressure.

3. Open with the natural release method—move the pressure cooker to a cool burner and wait for the pressure to come down on its own (about 10 minutes). For electric pressure cookers, disengage the "keep warm" mode or unplug the cooker and open when the pressure indicator has gone down (20–30 minutes).

4. Strain the stock through a fine mesh strainer. Store in the refrigerator for 2–3 days, or freeze for up to 3 months.

Fish Stock

Serves 12

1 pound fish heads, bones, and trimmings

6 black peppercorns

2 stalks celery, cut in two

1 carrot, peeled and cut in quarters

1 small white onion, peeled and quartered

1 bunch fresh parsley

7 cups cold water

1 cup dry (not sweet) white wine

1. Add all ingredients to the pressure cooker, pouring in enough water to bring the contents to the fill line. Bring to a boil, uncovered, over medium-high heat. When a boil is reached, skim and discard any foam from the surface. Close and lock the lid.

2. Turn the heat up to high. When the cooker reaches pressure, lower the heat to the minimum needed to maintain pressure. Cook for 10–12 minutes at high pressure.

3. Open with the natural release method—move the pressure cooker to a cool burner and wait for the pressure to come down on its own (about 10 minutes). For electric pressure cookers, disengage the "keep warm" mode or unplug the cooker and open when the pressure indicator has gone down (20–30 minutes).

4. Remove the lid and pour the stock through a fine mesh strainer, using a spatula to push on the remaining solids in the strainer to release their liquid. Discard the solids.

5. Cool and refrigerate for 1 day or freeze for up to 3 months.

Chicken Stock

Yield: 8 cups

1 tablespoon olive oil

2 pounds bone-in chicken pieces

1 bunch fresh parsley

2 carrots, peeled and cut in half

1 yellow onion, peeled and quartered

3 celery stalks, cut in half

1 bunch fresh thyme

1 tablespoon sea salt

6 cups water

1. Preheat the pressure cooker on low heat for 2–3 minutes, then add olive oil. When oil begins to simmer, add the chicken pieces. Turn the heat to medium and brown all of the chicken pieces well, turning frequently (about 7–10 minutes).

2. Add the parsley, carrots, onion, celery, thyme, and salt. Pour in just enough water to cover the vegetables. Close and lock the pressure cooker lid.

3. Turn the heat up to high. When the cooker reaches pressure, lower the heat to the minimum needed to maintain pressure. Cook for 20–25 minutes at high pressure.

4. Open with the natural release method—move the pressure cooker to a cool burner and wait for the pressure to come down on its own (about 10 minutes). For electric pressure cookers, disengage the "keep warm" mode or unplug the cooker and open when the pressure indicator has gone down (20–30 minutes).

5. Pour stock through a strainer into a large mixing bowl. Let the ingredients cool enough for you to pick through them and pull out any remaining chicken and vegetables. Set aside remaining chicken and vegetables to use with the broth as a chicken soup or as a filling for other recipes.

6. Let the liquid cool for about an hour before covering with plastic wrap. Refrigerate overnight.

Chicken Stock—continued

7. The next day, take the stock out of the refrigerator and spoon off the fat that has gathered at the top. If it has not solidified (it can depend on how much fat was on the pieces of chicken you used for the stock), you can remove the top layer by dropping a paper towel over the top and removing it as soon as it begins to absorb. You may need to do this several times to fully remove the top layer and clarify the stock.

8. Cool and refrigerate for 1 day or freeze for up to 3 months.

Beef Stock

Serves 12

1 tablespoon vegetable oil

1½ pounds bone-in chuck roast

1 pound cracked or sliced beef bones

1 large onion, peeled and quartered

2 large carrots, peeled and cut in two

2 stalks celery, cut in two

4 cups water, or to cover

1. In an uncovered pressure cooker, heat the vegetable oil over high heat. Brown the meat and bones on all sides. Reduce heat to medium and add the onion, carrots, celery, and enough water to cover all ingredients. Close and lock the lid.

2. Turn the heat up to high. When the cooker reaches pressure, lower the heat to the minimum needed to maintain pressure. Cook for 60–90 minutes at high pressure.

3. Open with the natural release method—move the pressure cooker to a cool burner and wait for the pressure to come down on its own (about 10 minutes). For electric pressure cookers, disengage the "keep warm" mode or unplug the cooker and open when the pressure indicator has gone down (20–30 minutes).

4. Strain or use a slotted spoon to remove the roast and beef bones. Reserve the roast and the meat removed from the bones for another use. Discard the bones.

5. Cool and refrigerate the broth overnight. The next day, take the stock out of the refrigerator and spoon off the fat that has gathered at the top.

6. Cool and refrigerate for 1 day or freeze for up to 3 months.

CHAPTER 5

Vegetables and Sides

Red Beans & Pork

Serves 8

1 cup dried red beans

6 cups water, divided

2 teaspoons olive or vegetable oil

2 pounds ham hocks

1 pound smoked sausage, diced

4 stalks celery, finely diced

1 large green bell pepper, seeded and diced

1 medium onion, peeled and diced

3 bay leaves

1 teaspoon freshly ground white pepper

1 teaspoon dried thyme

1 teaspoon garlic powder

1/4 teaspoon cayenne pepper

1/4 teaspoon freshly ground black pepper

Hot sauce, to taste

Salt, to taste

1. Wash and drain the beans; soak them overnight in 3 cups water.

2. Drain the beans and add them to the pressure cooker along with the remaining 3 cups of water and oil. Lock the lid into place and bring to low pressure; maintain pressure for 15 minutes. Remove from heat and allow pressure to release naturally for 10 minutes. Quick-release any remaining pressure and remove the lid.

3. Add the remaining ingredients except for the hot sauce and salt. Lock the lid into place and bring to high pressure; maintain pressure for 15 minutes. Remove from the heat and allow pressure to release naturally. Remove the lid.

4. Remove and discard the bay leaves. Remove the ham hocks; when cool enough to handle, remove the meat from the bones and stir into the beans. Discard any pork skin, fat, and bones. Taste for seasoning and add salt and hot sauce, to taste.

Macaroni & Cheese

Serves 6

1 tablespoon olive or vegetable oil

1 medium sweet onion, peeled and diced

1 clove garlic, peeled and minced

2 cups elbow macaroni

3 cups chicken broth

1 teaspoon salt

1/8 teaspoon freshly ground white pepper

1/2 cup whole milk

1/2 cup heavy cream

4 ounces Cheddar cheese, grated

4 ounces mozzarella cheese, grated

4 ounces Colby cheese, grated

1/4 cup dried bread crumbs

2 tablespoons butter, melted

1. Bring the oil to temperature in the pressure cooker over medium heat. Add the onion; sauté for 3 minutes or until the onion is soft. Add the garlic; sauté for 30 seconds. Add the macaroni and stir it to coat it in the oil. Stir in the broth, salt, and pepper. Lock the lid into place and bring to high pressure; maintain pressure for 6 minutes. Quick-release the pressure and remove the lid.

2. Preheat the oven to 350°F. Drain the macaroni. Transfer to a 9" × 13" ovenproof baking dish. Stir in the milk, cream, and cheeses. Mix the bread crumbs together with the melted butter and sprinkle over the top of the macaroni and cheese. Bake for 30 minutes or until the cheeses are melted and the bread crumbs are golden brown. Remove from the oven and let rest for 5 minutes. Serve.

Boston Baked Beans

Serves 8

1 pound dried small white beans

6 cups water

4 slices bacon, diced

2 medium sweet onions, peeled and diced

4 cloves garlic, peeled and minced

3$\frac{1}{2}$ cups chicken broth

2 teaspoons dried mustard

$\frac{1}{4}$ teaspoon freshly ground black pepper

$\frac{1}{4}$ cup molasses

$\frac{1}{2}$ cup ketchup

$\frac{1}{4}$ cup brown sugar

1 teaspoon Worcestershire sauce

1 teaspoon cider vinegar

Salt, to taste

Optional: Smoked paprika

1. Wash and drain the dried beans. Soak them overnight in 6 cups water, or enough to cover them by more than 1".

2. Fry the bacon in the pressure cooker over medium-high heat until the bacon begins to render its fat. Lower the heat to medium and add the onion; sauté for 3 minutes or until the onions are soft. Stir in the garlic; sauté for 30 seconds. Add the drained soaked beans, broth, dry mustard, and pepper.

3. Lock the lid into place and bring to low pressure; maintain pressure for 20 minutes. Remove from the heat and allow pressure to release naturally.

4. Remove the lid; the beans should still be somewhat soupy at this point. Stir in the molasses, ketchup, brown sugar, Worcestershire sauce, and vinegar. Stir to mix. Taste and add another $\frac{1}{4}$ cup of molasses if you prefer a heartier taste. Return the pan to the heat, lock the lid into place, and bring to low pressure; maintain pressure for 5 minutes. Remove from the heat and allow pressure to release naturally.

5. Remove the lid. Stir the beans and taste for seasoning. Add salt to taste and additional Worcestershire sauce if needed. If the beans are still too soupy, return to the heat and simmer them, stirring occasionally, until thickened. Stir in the smoked paprika if using. Serve.

Boston Baked Beans

Quinoa Artichoke Hearts Salad

Serves 4

1 cup pecans

1 cup uncooked quinoa

2$\frac{1}{2}$ cups water

2 cups frozen artichoke hearts

2 cups cherry or grape tomatoes, halved

2 shallots or $\frac{1}{2}$ small red onion, peeled and thinly sliced

$\frac{1}{4}$ cup Italian or Caesar salad dressing

2 heads Belgian endive

1. Rough chop the pecans and add them to the pressure cooker over medium heat. Dry roast for several minutes, stirring continuously to prevent the nuts from burning. The pecans are sufficiently toasted when they're fragrant and slightly brown. Transfer to a bowl and set aside to cool.

2. Add the quinoa and water to the pressure cooker. Lock the lid into place and bring to high pressure; maintain pressure for 2 minutes. Remove from the heat and allow pressure to release naturally for 10 minutes. Quick-release any remaining pressure. Transfer to a colander; drain and rinse under cold water. Drain well and transfer to a large bowl.

3. While the quinoa is cooking, prepare the artichoke hearts according to package direction and then plunge into cold water to cool and stop the cooking process. When cooled, cut into quarters.

4. Stir the artichoke hearts into the quinoa along with the tomatoes and shallots or red onion. Toss with the salad dressing. At this point, the quinoa mixture can be covered and refrigerated until ready to serve. This allows the flavors to blend. However, if you'll be refrigerating the quinoa mixture for more than 1 hour, leave the cherry or grape tomatoes whole rather than halving them.

5. To prepare the salad, separate the endive leaves. Rinse, drain, and divide them among four plates. Top each with one-fourth of the quinoa mixture. Sprinkle $\frac{1}{4}$ cup of the toasted pecans over the top of each salad.

Rice Pilaf

Serves 6–8

1½ tablespoons unsalted butter
1 medium carrot, peeled and grated
1 stalk celery, finely diced
1 medium onion, peeled and diced
2 cups long-grain white rice
¼ teaspoon salt
3 cups chicken broth

1. Melt the butter in the pressure cooker over medium heat. Add the carrot and celery; sauté for 3 minutes.

2. Add the onion; sauté for 3 minutes or until the onion is tender. Add the rice and stir into the vegetables. Add the salt and broth; stir.

3. Lock the lid into place and bring to high pressure; maintain pressure for 3 minutes. Remove from the heat and allow pressure to release naturally for 5 minutes.

4. Quick-release any remaining pressure and remove the lid. Fluff the rice with a fork. Serve.

Broccoli in Lemon Butter Sauce

Serves 6

4 cups broccoli florets
¼ teaspoon salt
1 cup water
4 tablespoons butter, melted
1 tablespoon fresh lemon juice
¼ teaspoon Dijon mustard

1. Put the broccoli, salt, and water in the pressure cooker. Lock the lid into place and bring to low pressure; maintain pressure for 2 minutes.

2. Remove the pressure cooker from the heat, quick-release the pressure, and remove the lid. Drain and transfer the broccoli to a serving bowl.

3. While the broccoli cooks, whisk together the butter, lemon juice, and mustard. Pour over the cooked broccoli and toss to mix.

Herb-Roasted Potatoes

Chapter 5: Vegetables and Sides

Herb-Roasted Potatoes

Serves 8

2 tablespoons olive oil

1 medium onion, peeled and diced

8 large red potatoes, scrubbed and quartered

¼ cup water

1 teaspoon Italian herb blend or Mrs. Dash Italian Medley Seasoning Blend

Salt and freshly ground black pepper, to taste

1. Bring the oil to temperature over medium heat in the pressure cooker. Add the onion; sauté for 3 minutes or until the onion is softened.

2. Add the potatoes, one of the cut sides down. Fry each side uncovered for 5 minutes or until the potatoes begin to brown.

3. Pour in the water. Sprinkle the herb blend over the potatoes. Season with salt and pepper.

4. Lock the lid into place and bring to high pressure; maintain pressure for 5 minutes. Remove from the heat and allow pressure to release naturally. Remove the lid. Serve.

Turnip and Carrot Purée

Serves 6

3 large turnips, peeled and quartered

4 large carrots, peeled and cut into 2-inch pieces

2 cups water

1 teaspoon salt; more for seasoning if needed

2 tablespoons extra-virgin olive oil

½ teaspoon nutmeg, freshly grated

2 tablespoons sour cream

1. Put turnips, carrots, water, and salt in pressure cooker. Lock lid into place and bring to high pressure; maintain pressure for 8 minutes. Remove pressure cooker from heat, quick-release pressure, and remove lid.

2. Drain vegetables. Return to the pressure cooker and put it over low heat for a minute or two to evaporate any residual moisture. Mash vegetables together with oil, nutmeg, and sour cream. Taste for seasoning and add additional salt if needed. Serve.

Mashed Rutabagas & Parsnips

Serves 4

1 (¾-pound) rutabaga, peeled, quartered, and sliced

2 parsnips, peeled and sliced

2 tablespoons butter

¼ teaspoon salt

¼ cup water

¼ cup heavy cream

¼ cup sour cream

Nutmeg, freshly grated

1. Add the rutabaga, parsnips, butter, salt, and water to the pressure cooker. Lock the lid into place and bring to low pressure; maintain pressure for 8 minutes.

2. Remove from heat and allow pressure to release naturally for 10 minutes. Quick-release any remaining pressure and remove the lid.

3. Drain any excess moisture from the vegetables or put the pressure cooker over low heat for a few minutes. Transfer to a food processor; pulse to purée the vegetables. Gradually add the heavy cream as you pulse the vegetables until they reach their desired consistency. Once the vegetables are puréed, transfer them to a serving bowl and stir in the sour cream. Taste for seasoning and add additional salt and sour cream if desired. Garnish with the nutmeg. Serve.

Thai Sweet Potatoes

Serves 6

2 tablespoons peanut or vegetable oil

1 red bell pepper, seeded and sliced

1 yellow bell pepper, seeded and sliced

1 orange bell pepper, seeded and sliced

1 large onion, peeled and sliced

2 cloves garlic, peeled and minced

1 tablespoon Thai green curry paste

3 large sweet potatoes, peeled and diced

1 (14-ounce) can unsweetened coconut milk

¼ cup water

1 teaspoon fresh lemon or lime juice

1½ cups snow peas or green beans

1½ tablespoons minced fresh cilantro

1. Bring the oil to temperature over medium heat. Add the bell pepper slices; sauté for 2 minutes.

2. Add the onion slices; sauté for 3 minutes or until the vegetables are soft. Add the garlic and curry paste; sauté for 1 minute.

3. Stir in the sweet potatoes, coconut milk, water, and lemon or lime juice. Lock the lid into place and bring to high pressure; maintain pressure for 3 minutes.

4. Remove the pressure cooker from heat, quick-release the pressure, and remove the lid. Taste for seasoning, adding more curry paste if desired.

5. Cut the snow peas or green beans into 1" segments. Stir into the sweet potato mixture in the pressure cooker.

6. Return the pressure cooker to medium heat and bring to a simmer. Maintain the simmer for 3 minutes or until the vegetables are cooked to tender-crisp. Stir in the cilantro. Serve.

Zesty Mashed Root Vegetables

Serves 8

1 cup water

2 pounds potatoes, peeled and diced

½ pound carrots, peeled and diced

1½ pounds white turnips, peeled and diced

1 teaspoon salt

4 tablespoons butter

1 cup heavy cream, divided

2 teaspoons prepared horseradish

Freshly ground black pepper, to taste

1. Add the water, potatoes, carrots, turnips, and salt to the pressure cooker in that order.

2. Lock the lid into place and bring to high pressure; maintain pressure for 7 minutes. Remove from the heat and allow pressure to release naturally for 10 minutes.

3. Quick-release any remaining pressure and remove the lid. Drain the vegetables and put them in a large serving bowl. Set aside and keep warm.

4. Wipe out the pressure cooker. Melt the butter and add ⅔ cup of the cream. Heat to low simmer over medium heat.

5. Mash the vegetables, stirring in the heated butter-cream mixture. Gradually add the remaining ⅓ cup of the cream if needed.

6. Stir in 1 teaspoon horseradish; taste for seasoning and add additional salt and the remaining horseradish if needed. Season to taste with pepper. Serve.

Asparagus with Olive Oil Dressing

Serves 4

1½ pounds fresh asparagus

½ cup water

2 tablespoons minced shallot or red onion

1 tablespoon fresh lemon juice

3 tablespoons extra-virgin olive oil

Salt and freshly ground white or black pepper, to taste

1. Clean the asparagus and snap off the ends. If necessary, peel the stems. Lay flat in the pressure cooker and add the water.

2. Lock the lid into place and bring to high pressure; maintain pressure for 3 minutes. Remove from the heat and allow pressure to release naturally for 2 minutes.

3. In a small bowl or measuring cup, whisk together the shallot or onion, lemon juice, oil, salt, and pepper.

4. Quick-release any remaining pressure and remove the lid. Drain the asparagus and transfer to a serving platter. Pour the dressing over the asparagus. Serve.

Mashed Turnips

Serves 4

4 medium turnips, peeled and diced

1 small onion, peeled and diced

$\frac{1}{2}$ cup beef or chicken broth

$\frac{1}{4}$ cup sour cream

Salt and freshly ground black pepper, to taste

1. Add the turnips, onion, and broth to the pressure cooker. Lock the lid into place and bring to high pressure; maintain pressure for 5 minutes. Remove from the heat and allow pressure to release naturally for 10 minutes.

2. Drain the turnips or use a slotted spoon to transfer them to a serving bowl. Use a handheld mixer or immersion blender to purée the turnips, adding some of the broth from the pressure cooker if necessary.

3. Stir in the sour cream. Taste for seasoning and add salt and pepper, to taste.

Mashed Turnips

Chapter 5: Vegetables and Sides

Celery with Lemon Butter Sauce

Serves 4

2 bunches celery

1 cup chicken broth

3 tablespoons butter, divided

1 tablespoon fresh lemon juice

Optional: 2 teaspoons rinsed and chopped capers; 1 tablespoon chopped fresh parsley

1. Remove the outer stalks from the celery. Cut off the ends and the tops. Quarter the remaining celery. Rinse, drain, and add to the pressure cooker with broth and 1 tablespoon butter. Lock the lid into place and bring to high pressure; maintain pressure for 5 minutes. Reduce to low pressure and maintain for 5 minutes. Remove from heat and allow pressure to release naturally for 5 minutes. Quick-release any remaining pressure and remove the lid. Use a slotted spoon to transfer the cooked celery to a serving platter; keep warm.

2. Discard all but ½ cup of the liquid in the pressure cooker. Return the pressure cooker to the heat and bring to a boil over medium-high heat. Boil until reduced by half. Stir in the lemon juice. Whisk in the remaining 2 tablespoons of butter a teaspoon at a time. Remove from heat. Stir in the capers and parsley if using. Pour over the celery. Serve.

Bavarian Kale

Serves 4

2 cups water

½ teaspoon salt

2 bunches kale, washed and drained

2 tablespoons olive or vegetable oil

1 small onion, peeled and diced

1 clove garlic, peeled and minced

1½ cups chicken broth

4 medium potatoes, peeled and diced

1 stalk celery, diced

Additional salt and freshly ground black pepper, to taste

Sour cream, for garnish

1. Add the water to the pressure cooker and bring to a boil over high heat. Stir in the salt. Cut the kale leaves into ½"-wide strips. Add the kale to the pressure cooker and blanch for 1 minute. Drain the kale in a colander and set aside.

2. Wipe out the pressure cooker and add the oil. Bring the oil to temperature in the pressure cooker over medium heat. Add the onion; sauté for 5 minutes or until it begins to brown. Add the garlic; sauté for 30 seconds.

3. Add the broth, potatoes, celery, and blanched kale. Lock the lid into place and bring to high pressure; maintain pressure for 6 minutes. Remove from the heat and allow pressure to release naturally. Remove the lid.

4. Stir, slightly mashing the potatoes into the mixture. Taste for seasoning and add additional salt and pepper, to taste. Garnish each serving with a dollop of sour cream.

Fennel Cooked in White Wine

Serves 4

4 fennel bulbs

1 tablespoon butter

1 tablespoon olive oil

1 small onion, peeled and diced

1 cup white wine

Salt and freshly ground black pepper,
    to taste

1. Cut off the tops and bottoms of the fennel bulbs and remove the two outer leaves. Thoroughly rinse the bulbs under cold running water. Dice the bulbs. Set aside.

2. Bring the butter and oil to temperature in the pressure cooker over medium heat. Add the onion; sauté for 3 minutes. Stir in the diced fennel; sauté for 3 minutes. Stir in the wine. Lock the lid into place and bring to low pressure; maintain pressure for 8 minutes.

3. Quick-release the pressure and remove the lid. Leave on the heat and simmer until the fennel is cooked through and soft and the alcohol is cooked out of the wine. This will mellow the flavor. Taste for seasoning and add salt and pepper, to taste. Serve.

Seasoned Baby Turnips

Serves 4

4 baby turnips

½ cup water

½ teaspoon salt

3 tablespoons butter

1 small onion, peeled and sliced

½ teaspoon sugar

¼ teaspoon freshly ground black pepper

¼ teaspoon ground allspice

2 tablespoons fresh lemon juice

Optional: 1 tablespoon minced fresh parsley

1. Clean, peel, and quarter the turnips. Place the rack in the pressure cooker. Pour in the water. Place the turnips on the rack and sprinkle them with the salt.

2. Lock the lid into place and bring to low pressure; maintain pressure for 8 minutes. Remove the pressure cooker from the heat, quick-release the pressure, and remove the lid.

3. Transfer the turnips to a serving bowl; set aside. Remove the rack and discard any water remaining in the pressure cooker. Wipe out the pressure cooker; add the butter and melt over medium heat. Add the onion; sauté for 3 minutes. Stir in the sugar, pepper, allspice, and lemon juice. Whisk and cook until the sugar is dissolved into the sauce. Add the turnips and toss to coat them in the sauce. Transfer back to the serving bowl. Sprinkle the parsley over the top if using.

Turnip Greens in Olive Oil

Serves 4

10 cups shredded turnip greens

½ cup chicken broth or water

1 clove garlic, peeled and crushed

½ teaspoon salt

4 teaspoons extra-virgin olive oil

Freshly ground black pepper, to taste

½ cup pecans, pine nuts, or pistachios, toasted

1. Rinse and drain the turnip greens. Add to the pressure cooker along with the broth or water, garlic, and salt.

2. Lock the lid into place and bring to low pressure; maintain pressure for 3 minutes. Remove from heat and allow pressure to release naturally for 5 minutes. Quick-release any remaining pressure and remove the lid.

3. Drain the turnip greens and transfer to a serving bowl. Toss with the oil. Add the pepper.

4. Taste for seasoning and add additional salt if needed. Stir in the toasted nuts. Serve.

Braised Beet Greens

Serves 4

1 tablespoon olive oil

1 large shallot or small red onion, peeled and minced

1 pound beet greens

Salt and freshly ground black pepper, to taste

¼ cup chicken broth or water

Optional: White wine or an infused vinegar

1. Bring the oil to temperature in the pressure cooker over medium heat. Add the shallot or onion; sauté for 3 minutes. Add the beet greens. Sprinkle with salt and pepper. Stir the greens to coat them in the oil. Once they're slightly wilted, add the broth or water, making sure not to exceed the fill line in your pressure cooker.

2. Lock the lid into place and bring to low pressure; maintain pressure for 1–3 minutes. Quick-release the pressure and remove the lid. Simmer and stir for a minute or until the remaining moisture in the pan evaporates. Taste for seasoning and add more salt and pepper if needed. Serve warm, with a splash of white wine or vinegar if desired.

CHAPTER 6

Sauces and Spreads

Tomato Chutney with Fresh Gingerroot

Yield: 2 pints

4 pounds ripe tomatoes, peeled
1 (1") piece fresh gingerroot
3 cloves garlic, peeled and minced
1¾ cups white sugar
1 cup red wine vinegar
2 onions, peeled and diced
¼ cup golden raisins
¾ teaspoon ground cinnamon
½ teaspoon ground coriander
¼ teaspoon ground cloves
¼ teaspoon ground nutmeg
¼ teaspoon ground ginger
1 teaspoon chili powder
⅛ teaspoon paprika
1 tablespoon curry paste

1. Purée the tomatoes and ginger in a blender or food processor. Transfer purée to pressure cooker and stir in remaining ingredients. Close and lock the lid.

2. Turn the heat up to high. When the cooker reaches pressure, lower the heat to the minimum needed to maintain pressure. Cook for 5–7 minutes at high pressure.

3. When time is up, open the pressure cooker by quick-releasing the pressure.

4. Refrigerate in a covered container until ready to use. Serve chilled or at room temperature.

Mango Chutney

Yield: 2 cups

2 almost ripe mangoes, peeled, pitted, and diced

2 small serrano or jalapeño peppers, seeded and minced

1 large clove garlic, peeled and minced

2 teaspoons grated, fresh ginger

6 unsweetened dried plums, coarsely chopped

¾ cup dark brown sugar, firmly packed

¾ cup raw sugar, or turbinado sugar

1 cup white wine vinegar

2 teaspoons mustard powder

⅛ teaspoon salt

1. Place all ingredients in the pressure cooker and stir to combine. Close and lock the lid.

2. Turn the heat up to high. When the cooker reaches pressure, lower the heat to the minimum needed to maintain pressure. Cook for 5 minutes at high pressure.

3. Open with the natural release method—move the pressure cooker to a cool burner and wait for the pressure to come down on its own (about 10 minutes). For electric pressure cookers, disengage the "keep warm" mode or unplug the cooker. After 10 minutes, release the rest of the pressure using the valve.

4. Remove the lid, return the pan to medium heat, and bring to a boil. Boil briskly for 10 minutes, stirring often. Cool thoroughly.

5. Cover and refrigerate overnight before using. Store covered in the refrigerator for up to 6 weeks.

Cranberry-Apple Chutney

Chapter 6: Sauces and Spreads

Cranberry-Apple Chutney

Serves 16

1 (12-ounce) bag cranberries

1 cup light brown sugar, packed

1 small sweet onion, peeled and diced

1 jalapeño pepper, seeded and minced

2 tablespoons fresh ginger, peeled and grated

1 clove garlic, peeled and minced

1 teaspoon yellow mustard seed

1 (3") stick of cinnamon

1 teaspoon lemon juice

¼ teaspoon salt

3 pounds tart cooking apples

Optional: Ground ginger to taste; ground cinnamon to taste

1. Rinse and pick over the cranberries. Add the cranberries, brown sugar, onion, jalapeño, ginger, garlic, mustard, cinnamon stick, lemon juice, and salt to a 5- to 7-quart pressure cooker. Cook over medium heat until the sugar dissolves, stirring occasionally.

2. Peel and core the apples; cut into strips, 1" in length. Place the apples in a layer over the cranberry mixture in the pressure cooker. Do not stir the apples into the mixture.

3. Lock the lid in place and bring to high pressure. Cook on high pressure for 1 minute. Remove from the heat and quick-release the pressure.

4. Remove the cinnamon stick. Taste for seasoning and add ground ginger and ground cinnamon if desired.

5. Store in a covered container in the refrigerator for up to 2 weeks. Serve heated or chilled.

Sausage and Mushroom Sauce

Yield: 5 cups

1 tablespoon olive oil

2 medium sweet onions, peeled and diced

8 ounces ground beef

1 pound Italian sausage

1 red bell pepper, seeded and diced

4 cloves garlic, peeled and minced

1 cup sliced mushrooms

1 medium carrot, peeled and grated

2½ teaspoons dried oregano

1 teaspoon dried basil

½ teaspoon fennel seed

1 teaspoon granulated cane sugar

1 bay leaf

1 (15-ounce) can plum tomatoes

2 cups tomato juice

½ cup red wine

¼ cup tomato paste

Salt and freshly ground black pepper, to taste

1. Bring the oil to temperature in the pressure cooker over medium-high heat. Add the onion and sauté for 2 minutes. Add the ground beef; fry for 5 minutes or until it renders its fat and loses its pink color. Drain and discard any fat.

2. Remove the casing from the Italian sausage; break the meat apart and add to the pressure cooker along with the bell pepper, garlic, mushrooms, and carrot. Sauté and stir for 3 minutes. Stir in the oregano, basil, fennel seed, and sugar. Add the bay leaf.

3. Dice or purée the plum tomatoes and juices in the blender. Stir into the meat mixture in the pressure cooker along with the tomato juice, wine, and tomato paste.

4. Lock the lid into place. Bring to high pressure; maintain for 20 minutes. Remove from the heat and quick-release the pressure.

5. Return to the heat; stir and simmer the sauce uncovered for a few minutes to thicken it. Taste for seasoning and add salt and pepper if needed.

Mixed Citrus Marmalade

Yield: 4 cups

1 large orange
1 lime
2 lemons
2 clementines or satsumas
1 pink grapefruit
3 cups water, divided
4 pounds jam sugar

1. Wash the fruit in hot water to remove any wax. Remove the zest from the orange, lime, and lemons; add to the pressure cooker. Quarter all fruit and place in a large (doubled) piece of cheesecloth; twist the cheesecloth to squeeze out the juice into the pressure cooker. Tie the cheesecloth over the fruit and seeds and add it to the pressure cooker along with half of the water. Lock the lid in place and bring the pressure cooker to high pressure; cook on high for 10 minutes. Remove from the heat and allow pressure to release naturally.

2. Remove the lid from the pressure cooker. Place the cooker over medium heat and add the remaining water and sugar. Bring to a boil, stirring continuously until all the sugar has dissolved.

3. While the mixture continues to boil, place the lid back on the cooker (but do not lock it into place). Leave the lid in place for 2 minutes, remove it, and then continue to let the mixture boil for 8 minutes or until the desired gel point is reached.

4. Skim off and discard any foam. Ladle into hot, sterilized glass containers or jars, leaving ½" of head space. Seal the containers or jars. Cool and refrigerate for a week or freeze until needed. (If you prefer, you can follow the instructions that came with your canning jars and process the preserves for shelf storage.)

Wild Berry Black Currant Jam

Yield: 3 cups

3 cups cranberries

3 cups hulled and diced strawberries

1 cup blueberries

¼ cup diced rhubarb stalk

¼ cup dried black currants

Zest and juice of 1 lemon

3 cups granulated sugar

2 tablespoons water

⅛ teaspoon sea salt

1. Add the cranberries, strawberries, blueberries, rhubarb stalk, currants, lemon zest, and lemon juice to the pressure cooker. Stir in the sugar. Set aside for 1 hour, until the fruit is juicy.

2. Stir in the water and sea salt. Close and lock the lid.

3. Turn the heat up to high. When the cooker reaches pressure, lower the heat to the minimum needed to maintain pressure. Cook for 8–10 minutes at high pressure.

4. Open with the natural release method—move the pressure cooker to a cool burner and wait for the pressure to come down on its own (about 10 minutes). For electric pressure cookers, disengage the "keep warm" mode or unplug the cooker. After 10 minutes, release the rest of the pressure using the valve.

5. Remove the lid and purée the contents using an immersion blender. Return to medium heat and bring to a full boil, stirring constantly for 3 minutes or until jam reaches the desired gel state.

6. Skim off and discard any foam. Ladle into hot, sterilized, glass containers or jars, leaving ½" of headspace. Seal the containers or jars. Cool and refrigerate for a week or freeze.

Wild Berry Black Currant Jam

Chapter 6: Sauces and Spreads

Sweet Onion Relish

Yield: 4 cups

4 medium sweet onions
Water
¾ cup golden raisins
1 cup honey
1 tablespoon cider vinegar
Pinch salt

1. Peel and thinly slice onions. Add onions to the pressure cooker and pour in enough water to cover. Bring to a boil over high heat; drain immediately and discard water.

2. Return onions to pressure cooker; stir in raisins, honey, vinegar, and salt until honey is evenly distributed throughout onion slices.

3. Lock on lid, bring to high pressure, and cook for 5 minutes. Reduce heat and maintain low pressure for an additional 10 minutes. Remove from heat and allow pressure to release naturally.

4. Remove lid and stir relish. If relish needs thickening, return pan to heat, bring to a gentle boil, and boil for 5 minutes or until desired thickness is reached. Can be served warm or stored in a covered container in the refrigerator for up to 4 weeks.

Apple Butter

Yield: About 2 cups

1 cup apple juice or cider

12 medium apples (about 3 pounds)

1½ teaspoons ground cinnamon

½ teaspoon ground allspice

⅛ teaspoon ground cloves

1½ cups sugar

Optional: 1 or 2 drops oil of cinnamon

1. Add the apple juice or cider to the pressure cooker. Wash, peel, core, and dice the apples and add to the pressure cooker.

2. Lock the lid into place, bring to high pressure, and immediately remove from heat; let the pressure release naturally for 10 minutes. Quick-release any remaining pressure.

3. Once the apples have cooled, press through a fine sieve or food mill, or process in a food processor or blender. Return the apples and cooking liquids to the pressure cooker and stir in the cinnamon, allspice, cloves, sugar, and oil of cinnamon if using.

4. Return the pan to medium heat and bring to a simmer. Simmer uncovered and stir until the sugar is dissolved and reduce heat.

5. Continue to simmer and stir for 1 hour or until the mixture is very thick. Note that it's important that you frequently stir the apple butter from the bottom of the pan to prevent it from burning.

6. Cool and refrigerate covered for up to 10 days or freeze for up to 4 months.

Vanilla-Spice Pear Butter

Yield: 2 cups

6 medium Bartlett pears

¼ cup dry white wine, such as Sauvignon Blanc

Zest and juice of 1 lemon

¾ cup sugar

2 orange slices

1 lemon slice

2 whole cloves

1 vanilla bean, split lengthwise

1 cinnamon stick

¼ teaspoon ground cardamom

⅛ teaspoon salt

1. Rinse, peel, and core the pears, then dice them into 1" pieces. Add the pears, wine, lemon zest, and lemon juice to the pressure cooker. Close and lock the lid.

2. Turn the heat up to high. When the cooker reaches pressure, lower the heat to the minimum needed to maintain pressure. Cook for 5 minutes at high pressure.

3. Open with the natural release method—move the pressure cooker to a cool burner and wait for the pressure to come down on its own (about 10 minutes). For electric pressure cookers, disengage the "keep warm" mode or unplug the cooker. After 10 minutes, release the rest of the pressure using the valve.

4. Purée the contents of the cooker using an immersion blender. Add the sugar. Stir and cook over low heat until sugar dissolves, about 3 minutes.

5. Stir in the remaining ingredients. Increase the heat to medium and boil gently, cooking and stirring for about 30 minutes or until mixture thickens and mounds slightly on spoon.

6. Remove and discard the orange and lemon slices, cloves, and cinnamon stick. Remove the vanilla pod; use the back of a knife to scrape away any vanilla seeds still clinging to the pod and stir them into the pear butter.

7. Cool and refrigerate covered for up to 10 days or freeze for up to 4 months.

Fresh Tomato Sauce

Yield: 4 cups

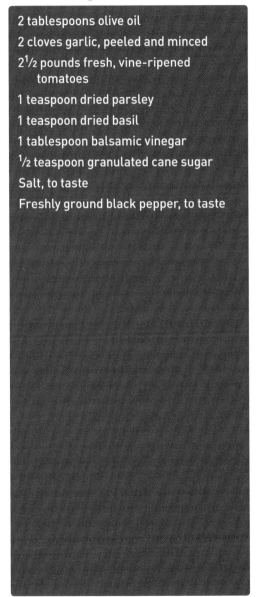

2 tablespoons olive oil

2 cloves garlic, peeled and minced

2½ pounds fresh, vine-ripened tomatoes

1 teaspoon dried parsley

1 teaspoon dried basil

1 tablespoon balsamic vinegar

½ teaspoon granulated cane sugar

Salt, to taste

Freshly ground black pepper, to taste

1. Add the oil to the pressure cooker and bring to temperature over medium heat. Add the garlic; sauté for 30 seconds.

2. Peel and dice the tomatoes. Add them to the pressure cooker along with the tomato juice and the remaining ingredients.

3. Lock the lid in place and bring to low pressure; maintain for 10 minutes. Remove from the heat and allow pressure to release naturally.

4. Remove the lid and stir the sauce. If you prefer a thicker sauce, return to the heat and simmer uncovered for 10 minutes or until it reaches the desired thickness.

Lemon Custard

Chapter 6: Sauces and Spreads

Lemon Custard

Serves 6

½ cup sugar
1 tablespoon cornstarch
2 large eggs
2 egg yolks
1½ cups milk
1 cup heavy cream
2 medium lemons
2 cups water

1. Add the sugar and cornstarch to a bowl. Stir to combine well. Whisk in the eggs and egg yolks. Stir in the milk and cream. Grate the zest from one of the lemons and add it to the batter along with the juice from both lemons (about ¼ cup). Evenly divide among six ½-cup custard cups. Tightly cover the top of each custard cup with aluminum foil to prevent any water from getting into the cups.

2. Set the rack in the bottom of the pressure cooker and pour in the water. Place the custard cups on the rack, stacking them if you need to.

3. Lock the lid into place and bring to high pressure; maintain pressure for 12 minutes. Remove the pressure cooker from the heat, quick-release the pressure, and remove the lid.

4. Carefully lift the custard cups from the pressure cooker and place them on a wire rack. Remove the foil.

5. Let custard cool to room temperature. Once cooled, cover each cup with plastic wrap and chill overnight in refrigerator.

Quick Demi-Glace

Yield: 1 cup

1½ pounds veal bones

1½ pounds beef bones

1 pound chicken backs

Water

1 tablespoon vegetable oil

1 medium white onion, peeled and diced

1 large carrot, peeled and diced

1 celery stalk with leaves, diced

1 tablespoon dried parsley

½ teaspoon dried thyme

½ teaspoon whole black peppercorns

1 bay leaf

1. Trim the bones of any fat, but leave some meat attached to them. Discard any chicken skin and chop the backs into 3" pieces.

2. Preheat the broiler. Arrange the veal and beef bones in a roasting pan; place the pan in the oven about 6" away from the source of heat. Broil for 15 minutes. Remove the roasting pan from the oven and turn the bones. Add the chopped chicken backs to the pan and return the pan to the oven. Broil for another 15 minutes.

3. Pour off and discard the rendered fat from the roasting pan. Place the pan over two burners on medium-high heat until the pan sizzles. Pour in 2 cups of water and stir it into the bones, scraping up the browned bits on the bottom of the roasting pan. Remove from heat.

4. Add the oil to the pressure cooker and bring to temperature. Stir in the onion, carrot, celery, parsley, thyme, and peppercorns; sauté for 3 minutes. Add the bay leaf. Transfer the broiled bones and water to the pressure cooker. If necessary, add additional hot water so that the water level is 1" above the bones. (Note: The bones and water should not fill the pressure cooker beyond two-thirds full. If you're using a small pressure cooker, you'll need to divide the bones and cook the bones in two batches.)

5. Lock the lid into place and bring to high pressure; maintain for 1½ hours. Remove from the heat and allow pressure to release naturally. Strain the stock into a stockpot.

6. Let rest for 10 minutes and then skim off and discard any fat. Place the stockpot over high heat and bring to a boil. Reduce the heat, but maintain and boil for an hour or until the liquid is dark brown and thick; it should be evaporated to about 1 cup at this point. Chilled demi-glace can be cut into cubes, wrapped in plastic, and stored in the refrigerator for 2 weeks, and can be frozen indefinitely in freezer bags.

Memphis-Style Barbecue Sauce

Yield: 4 cups

2 cups ketchup

1 1/2 cups distilled white vinegar

1/4 cup light brown sugar

2 tablespoons onion powder

1/4 cup Worcestershire sauce

1/4 cup prepared mustard

1 teaspoon freshly ground black pepper

Salt, to taste

Optional: Cayenne pepper or hot sauce, to taste

Add all ingredients except the salt and cayenne pepper or hot sauce to the pressure cooker. Lock on the lid and bring to low pressure; maintain pressure for 5 minutes. Quick-release the pressure. Stir the sauce and taste for seasoning; add salt and cayenne pepper or hot sauce if desired. Allow sauce to cool and then refrigerate in a covered container for up to a week or freeze until needed.

Spicy Eggplant Sauce

Serves 6

1 tablespoon olive oil
¼ teaspoon hot pepper flakes
2 anchovies
1 clove garlic, peeled and smashed
2 large eggplants, diced
1 teaspoon salt
¼ teaspoon black pepper
⅔ cup water
1 sprig of fresh oregano

1. In the cold pressure cooker, add the oil, pepper flakes, anchovies, and garlic. Turn on low heat to infuse the oil with these flavors until the garlic begins to sizzle and the anchovies fall apart, about 3 minutes.

2. Separate the diced eggplant into two piles. Turn the heat up to medium and add half of the eggplant into the pressure cooker, uncovered. Add salt and pepper to taste.

3. Stir the eggplant around, lightly browning it on most sides for about 5 minutes. Add the remaining eggplant. Mix everything well, add water, and rest the oregano sprig on top. Close and lock the lid.

4. Turn the heat up to high. When the cooker reaches pressure, lower the heat to the minimum needed to maintain pressure. Cook for 3–5 minutes at high pressure.

5. When time is up, open the pressure cooker by quick-releasing the pressure.

6. Discard the herb sprig and pour the contents on freshly strained pasta, or if using as a side dish, remove the eggplant to a serving dish immediately to stop it from cooking further and falling apart.

Mixed Pepper Sauce

Serves 6

1 tablespoon olive oil

2 red peppers, seeded and thinly sliced into strips

2 yellow peppers, seeded and thinly sliced into strips

1 green pepper, seeded and thinly sliced into strips

1 red onion, peeled and thinly sliced

4 Roma-type tomatoes, peeled and puréed (or 1 cup canned chopped tomatoes)

1 garlic clove, peeled and pressed

1 bunch fresh parsley, chopped

1. Heat olive oil in an uncovered pressure cooker over medium heat. Add peppers and onion. Stir infrequently until one side is lightly browned (about 5 minutes). Add the tomatoes and their liquid. Close and lock the lid.

2. Turn the heat up to high. When the cooker reaches pressure, lower the heat to the minimum needed to maintain pressure. Cook for 3–5 minutes at high pressure.

3. When time is up, open the pressure cooker by quick-releasing the pressure.

4. Add the garlic and parsley and purée using an immersion blender.

Dried Plum Sauce

Serves 12

7 ounces dried plums, pitted

1 tablespoon brown sugar

$\frac{1}{8}$ onion, peeled and sliced

1 teaspoon minced or grated ginger

1 teaspoon minced, fresh red chili

1 clove garlic, peeled and minced

$\frac{2}{3}$ cup water

2 tablespoons rice wine vinegar

1. Add all ingredients except vinegar to pressure cooker, then close and lock the lid.

2. Turn the heat up to high. When the cooker reaches pressure, lower the heat to the minimum needed to maintain pressure. Cook for 5–7 minutes at high pressure.

3. When time is up, open the pressure cooker by quick-releasing the pressure.

4. Add the vinegar and purée the contents of the pressure cooker using an immersion blender.

5. On low heat, stir frequently until the contents have reached sauce consistency (about 5 minutes).

Light Mushroom Cream Sauce

Serves 6

1 tablespoon olive oil

2 tablespoons butter, divided

1 pound button mushrooms, roughly sliced

1 bunch parsley, stems and leaves divided and chopped

1 cup vegetable broth

2 ounces dried porcini mushrooms, crumbled

1/2 teaspoon salt

1/4 teaspoon white pepper

1 tablespoon flour

1 cup whole milk

1/4 teaspoon nutmeg

1. Heat olive oil and 1 tablespoon butter in an uncovered pressure cooker over medium heat. Sauté button mushrooms and parsley stems, stirring infrequently until mushrooms are lightly browned (about 8–10 minutes). Add the broth, porcini mushrooms, salt, and pepper. Mix well. Close and lock the lid.

2. Turn the heat up to high. When the cooker reaches pressure, lower the heat to the minimum needed to maintain pressure. Cook for 5 minutes at high pressure.

3. When time is up, open the pressure cooker by quick-releasing the pressure.

4. Mix in flour, milk, and nutmeg. Purée sauce using an immersion blender.

5. Simmer sauce on low heat until desired consistency is reached.

6. Sprinkle with parsley leaves before serving.

Quick Sausage Ragu

Serves 6

8 ounces Italian sausage, removed from casing

1 red onion, peeled and chopped

1 clove garlic, peeled and pressed

3 sprigs of fresh oregano, chopped

¼ teaspoon salt

⅛ teaspoon black pepper

1 (14½-ounce) can chopped tomatoes

1. In the cold pressure cooker, add the crumbled Italian sausage, then set the heat to low to slowly melt and render the fat. Stir the sausage to break it up and then add the onion and raise the heat to medium-high. Sauté for 5 minutes or until the onion begins to soften. Add garlic, oregano, salt, pepper, and tomatoes. Stir well, scraping the bottom to remove and incorporate any browned bits that may have gotten stuck. Close and lock the lid.

2. Turn the heat up to high. When the cooker reaches pressure, lower the heat to the minimum needed to maintain pressure. Cook for 5–6 minutes at high pressure.

3. Open with the natural release method—move the pressure cooker to a cool burner and wait for the pressure to come down on its own (about 10 minutes). For electric pressure cookers, disengage the "keep warm" mode or unplug the cooker. After 10 minutes, release the rest of the pressure using the valve.

4. Pour over freshly strained pasta, mix, and serve.

Bolognese Meat Sauce

Serves 6

4 ounces pancetta, cubed

1 onion, peeled and chopped

1 carrot, peeled and chopped

1 celery stalk, chopped

11 ounces ground beef

½ cup of Sangiovese, or other dry red wine

5 tablespoons tomato paste

1 cup Beef Stock (see recipe in Chapter 4)

½ teaspoon salt

¼ teaspoon black pepper

1 tablespoon heavy cream

1. In the cold pressure cooker, place the pancetta in a flat layer and turn on the lowest possible heat to render the fat. When the pancetta begins to sizzle, raise heat to medium-high and add the onion, carrot, and celery. Sauté until the onions have softened (about 5 minutes). If the ingredients begin to stick, you can add a tablespoon of water.

2. Add ground beef and brown well, stirring occasionally until all of the liquid is evaporated and the fat begins to sizzle (about 20–30 minutes).

3. Add the wine, scraping the bits stuck to the bottom and sides of the pan, and evaporate it completely (about 7 minutes). In the meantime, mix the tomato paste with the beef stock, salt, and pepper. Add stock mixture to the pan and stir well, scraping the bottom of the pan. Close and lock the lid.

4. Turn the heat up to high. When the cooker reaches pressure, lower the heat to the minimum needed to maintain pressure. Cook for 18–20 minutes at high pressure.

5. Open with the natural release method—move the pressure cooker to a cool burner and wait for the pressure to come down on its own (about 10 minutes). For electric pressure cookers, disengage the "keep warm" mode or unplug the cooker. After 10 minutes, release the rest of the pressure using the valve.

6. Stir in the cream and serve.

CHAPTER 7

Poultry Entrées

Pesto Chicken

Serves 4

3 pounds bone-in chicken thighs

1/3 cup pesto

1/2 cup chicken broth

1 large sweet onion, peeled and sliced

8 small red potatoes, peeled

1 (1-pound) bag baby carrots

1. Remove the skin and trim the chicken thighs of any fat; add to a large zip-closure bag along with the pesto. Seal and shake to coat the chicken in the pesto.

2. Add the broth and onions to the pressure cooker. Place the trivet or cooking rack on top of the onions. Arrange the chicken on the rack and then add the potatoes and carrots to the top of the chicken.

3. Lock the lid into place. Bring to high pressure; maintain pressure for 11 minutes.

4. Remove the pressure cooker from the heat. Quick-release the pressure. Transfer the chicken, potatoes, and carrots to a serving platter. Use tongs to remove the trivet or cooking rack.

5. Remove any fat from the juices remaining in the pan, then strain the juices over the chicken and vegetables. Serve hot.

Chicken Bordeaux

Serves 4

3 tablespoons vegetable oil

1 clove garlic, peeled and crushed

3 pounds chicken pieces

1 teaspoon cracked black pepper

1 cup dry white wine

1 (15-ounce) can diced tomatoes

4 ounces mushrooms, sliced

1. Bring the oil to temperature in the pressure cooker over medium-high heat. Add garlic; sauté to infuse the garlic flavor into the oil. Remove garlic and discard.

2. Rub chicken with pepper. Arrange the chicken pieces skin side down in the pressure cooker. Pour in the wine and tomatoes. Add the mushrooms.

3. Lock the lid into place and bring to low pressure; maintain for 10 minutes. Remove from the heat and quick-release the pressure.

4. Remove chicken to a serving platter and keep warm. Return the pressure cooker to the heat and simmer the sauce until it thickens. Pour over the chicken.

Curried Chicken Salad

Serves 6

1 medium sweet onion, peeled and quartered

1 large carrot, peeled and diced

1 stalk celery, diced

8 peppercorns

1 cup water

3 pounds chicken breast halves, bone-in and with skin

1/4 cup mayonnaise

1/2 cup sour cream

2–3 tablespoons curry powder

Salt, to taste

1/2 teaspoon freshly ground black pepper

1 1/2 cups peeled and diced apples

1/2 cup seedless green grapes, halved

1 cup sliced celery

1 cup slivered almonds, toasted

2 tablespoons diced red onion or shallot

1. Add the onion, carrot, celery, peppercorns, water, and chicken to the pressure cooker.

2. Lock the lid into place and bring to high pressure; maintain pressure for 10 minutes.

3. Remove from heat; allow pressure to release naturally for 10 minutes and then quick-release any remaining pressure.

4. Use a slotted spoon to transfer chicken to a bowl. Strain the broth in the pressure cooker and then pour it over the chicken. Allow chicken to cool in the broth.

5. To make the salad, add the mayonnaise, sour cream, curry powder, salt, and pepper to a bowl. Stir to mix. Stir in the apples, grapes, celery, almonds, and red onion or shallot.

6. Remove the chicken from the bones. Discard the bones and skin. Dice the chicken and fold into the salad mixture. Chill until ready to serve.

Ginger-Chili Chicken

Serves 6

1 cup plain yogurt

1 clove garlic, peeled and minced

2 teaspoons grated fresh ginger

¼ teaspoon cayenne pepper

3 pounds boneless, skinless chicken thighs

1 (15-ounce) can diced tomatoes

8 teaspoons ketchup

½ teaspoon chili powder

4 tablespoons butter

1 teaspoon sugar

½ cup cashews, crushed

Salt and freshly ground black pepper, to taste

Optional: Plain yogurt or sour cream; a few drops of red coloring

1. Mix together the yogurt, garlic, ginger, and cayenne pepper in a bowl or zip-closure bag; add the chicken thighs and marinate for 4 hours.

2. Remove the chicken thighs from the marinade and add them to the pressure cooker along with the undrained diced tomatoes, ketchup, and chili powder.

3. Lock the lid into place and bring to low pressure; maintain pressure for 8 minutes. Quick-release the pressure.

4. Use a slotted spoon to move cooked chicken thighs to a serving platter and keep warm.

5. Use an immersion blender to purée the tomatoes. Whisk in the butter and sugar. Stir in the cashews. Taste for seasoning and add salt and pepper, to taste.

6. If the sauce is spicier than you'd like, stir in some plain yogurt or sour cream 1 tablespoon at a time until you're pleased with the taste. Add red food coloring if desired. Pour over the chicken thighs and serve.

Herbed Chicken in Lemon Sauce

Serves 4

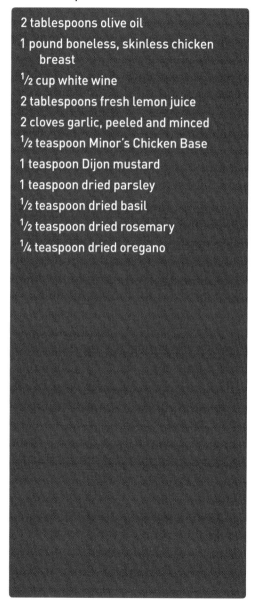

2 tablespoons olive oil

1 pound boneless, skinless chicken breast

1/2 cup white wine

2 tablespoons fresh lemon juice

2 cloves garlic, peeled and minced

1/2 teaspoon Minor's Chicken Base

1 teaspoon Dijon mustard

1 teaspoon dried parsley

1/2 teaspoon dried basil

1/2 teaspoon dried rosemary

1/4 teaspoon dried oregano

1. Bring the oil to temperature in the pressure cooker over medium heat. Cut the chicken into bite-sized pieces. Add to the pressure cooker; stir-fry for 5 minutes.

2. Add the remaining ingredients; mix well. Lock the lid into place and bring to low pressure; maintain for 10 minutes. Remove from heat and quick-release pressure.

3. If the sauce needs thickening, use a slotted spoon to transfer the chicken to a serving bowl and keep warm. Return the pan to the heat and simmer, uncovered, for 5 to 10 minutes. Pour the sauce over the chicken and serve.

Herbed Chicken in Lemon Sauce

Chicken with Mushrooms in White Wine

Serves 6

1 tablespoon olive oil

1 clove garlic, peeled and crushed

3 pounds bone-in chicken pieces

1 teaspoon cracked black pepper

$\frac{1}{2}$ cup dry white wine

1 (15-ounce) can diced tomatoes

4 ounces mushrooms, sliced

2 teaspoons salt

1. Heat olive oil in an uncovered pressure cooker over medium heat. Sauté the garlic until golden (about 1 minute).

2. Rub chicken with pepper. Arrange the chicken pieces skin side down in the pressure cooker and brown well (approximately 5 minutes). You may need to work in batches.

3. Remove chicken from pan and deglaze the bottom with wine until the liquid is almost completely evaporated (about 3 minutes). Arrange all pieces skin side up in the pressure cooker, then add tomatoes, mushrooms, and salt. Close and lock the lid.

4. Turn the heat up to high. When the cooker reaches pressure, lower the heat to the minimum needed to maintain pressure. Cook for 8–10 minutes at high pressure.

5. When time is up, open the pressure cooker by quick-releasing the pressure.

6. Transfer chicken to a serving platter and keep warm.

7. In the uncovered pressure cooker, reduce the sauce until thickened. Pour over chicken and serve.

Spicy Ginger Chicken

Serves 6

1 tablespoon vegetable oil

1 teaspoon grated fresh ginger

3 cloves garlic, peeled and minced

½ teaspoon crushed red pepper flakes

1 teaspoon white pepper

3 pounds skinless, bone-in chicken pieces

1 tablespoon soy sauce

1 tablespoon honey

¾ cup water

1. Heat oil in an uncovered pressure cooker over medium heat. Sauté the ginger, garlic, crushed red pepper, and white pepper for about 2 minutes. Add the chicken pieces and drizzle with soy sauce and honey. Add the water. Close and lock the lid.

2. Turn the heat up to high. When the cooker reaches pressure, lower the heat to the minimum needed to maintain pressure. Cook for 8–10 minutes at high pressure.

3. When time is up, open the pressure cooker by quick-releasing the pressure.

4. Remove the chicken pieces to a serving platter and cover loosely with foil. Reduce the liquid in the uncovered cooker over medium-high heat to ¼ of its amount, or until it becomes thick and syrupy.

5. Pour reduced pan juices over chicken and serve.

Whole Beer-Can Chicken

Serves 6

2 tablespoons chopped fresh rosemary (reserve a teaspoon for garnish)

2 tablespoons chopped fresh sage

2 tablespoons chopped fresh thyme

2 tablespoons olive oil

Juice and zest of 1 lemon

1 teaspoon salt

$\frac{1}{2}$ teaspoon black pepper

1 (3$\frac{1}{2}$-pound) chicken

1 can beer (your choice)

2 bay leaves, divided

1. In a bowl, prepare the seasoning by mixing the rosemary, sage, thyme, olive oil, lemon juice, salt, and pepper.

2. Rinse chicken inside and out and pat dry. Tuck the tips of the wings behind the neck opening of the chicken and brush on the seasoning. In a separate pan brown the seasoned chicken well on all sides.

3. Pour $\frac{1}{3}$ of the beer out of the can and place half the lemon zest and one bay leaf into the can. Place the can in the middle of the pressure cooker. Lower the chicken over the can of beer so that the can is inside the cavity. Pour any of the remaining seasoning and liquid from the sauté pan over the chicken. Add the remaining lemon zest and bay leaf to the pressure cooker. Close and lock the lid.

4. Turn the heat up to high. When the cooker reaches pressure, lower the heat to the minimum needed to maintain pressure. Cook for 20–25 minutes at high pressure.

5. Open with the natural release method—move the pressure cooker to a cool burner and wait for the pressure to come down on its own (about 10 minutes). For electric pressure cookers, disengage the "keep warm" mode or unplug the cooker. After 10 minutes, release the rest of the pressure using the valve.

6. Carefully remove the chicken and the beer can from the pressure cooker. Place the chicken on the serving platter to rest tented with aluminum foil, pour in the remaining beer from the can and discard. Simmer the contents of the uncovered cooker for about 5 minutes or until reduced by $\frac{1}{2}$. Strain the pan sauce and pour over the chicken. Sprinkle with fresh rosemary before serving.

Petit Turkey Meatloaf

Serves 4

1 pound lean ground turkey
1 onion, peeled and diced
1 stalk celery, minced
1 carrot, peeled and grated
½ cup butter cracker crumbs
½ cup grated Pecorino Romano cheese
1 clove garlic, peeled and minced
1 teaspoon chopped fresh basil
1 teaspoon mustard
1 teaspoon sea salt
¼ teaspoon black pepper
1 large egg
3 tablespoons ketchup
1 cup water

1. Add all ingredients except the water to a large bowl and mix well. Divide the mixture between two mini loaf pans. Pack the mixture down into the pans.

2. Place water in the pressure cooker and add the steamer basket. Lower the little pans onto the basket. Close and lock the lid.

3. Turn the heat up to high. When the cooker reaches pressure, lower the heat to the minimum needed to maintain pressure. Cook for 15–20 minutes at high pressure.

4. Open with the natural release method—move the pressure cooker to a cool burner and wait for the pressure to come down on its own (about 10 minutes). For electric pressure cookers, disengage the "keep warm" mode or unplug the cooker and open when the pressure indicator has gone down (20–30 minutes).

5. Use oven mitts or tongs to lift the pans out of the pressure cooker. Serve directly from the pans or transfer to a serving platter.

Herbed Turkey Breast with Mushroom Gravy

Herbed Turkey Breast with Mushroom Gravy

Serves 6

1 tablespoon vegetable oil

3 tablespoons butter, divided

1 large sweet onion, peeled and diced

1 pound fresh mushrooms, sliced

4 cloves garlic, peeled and minced

2 teaspoons Mrs. Dash Garlic & Herb Seasoning Blend

1 (2-pound) boneless rolled turkey breast

1¾ cups chicken or turkey broth

½ cup sweet Madeira or Port wine

1 bay leaf

¼ cup all-purpose flour

Salt and freshly ground black pepper, to taste

1. Bring the oil and 1 tablespoon of the butter to temperature in the pressure cooker over medium-high heat. Add the onion; sauté for 3 minutes or until transparent. Add the mushrooms; sauté for 3 minutes. Stir in the Mrs. Dash garlic and herb blend. Push the sautéed vegetables to the sides of the pan and add the turkey breast.

2. Cook the turkey for 3 minutes or until it browns on the bottom; turn the turkey over and fry for another 3 minutes. Use tongs to lift the turkey out of the pressure cooker. Spread the sautéed mixture over the bottom of the pot, and then insert the cooking rack. Nestle the turkey on the rack. Add the broth, Madeira or Port, and bay leaf.

3. Lock the lid into place. Bring to low pressure; maintain low pressure for 25 minutes. Remove from the heat and allow pressure to release naturally.

4. Remove the lid and transfer the turkey to a serving platter. Tent the turkey in aluminum foil and let it rest for at least 10 minutes before you carve it.

5. Remove and discard the bay leaf. Skim off any excess fat from the top of the broth. In a small bowl or measuring cup, mix the remaining butter together with the flour. Stir in some of the broth to form a paste.

6. Bring the pan juices in the pressure cooker to a boil over medium-high heat. Stir in the flour mixture; lower the temperature to maintain a simmer and stir and cook for 3 minutes or until the gravy is thickened. Taste for seasoning and add salt and pepper if needed. Pour into a gravy boat.

Citrus Spice Chicken

Serves 6

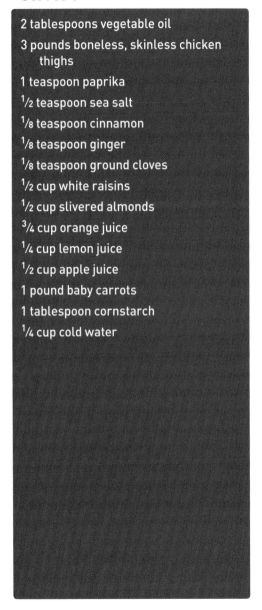

2 tablespoons vegetable oil

3 pounds boneless, skinless chicken thighs

1 teaspoon paprika

1/2 teaspoon sea salt

1/8 teaspoon cinnamon

1/8 teaspoon ginger

1/8 teaspoon ground cloves

1/2 cup white raisins

1/2 cup slivered almonds

3/4 cup orange juice

1/4 cup lemon juice

1/2 cup apple juice

1 pound baby carrots

1 tablespoon cornstarch

1/4 cup cold water

1. Heat olive oil in an uncovered pressure cooker over medium heat. Fry chicken thighs for 2 minutes on each side. Add the paprika, salt, cinnamon, ginger, cloves, raisins, almonds, orange juice, lemon juice, apple juice, and carrots. Close and lock the lid.

2. Turn the heat up to high. When the cooker reaches pressure, lower the heat to the minimum needed to maintain pressure. Cook for 8–10 minutes at high pressure.

3. When time is up, open the pressure cooker by quick-releasing the pressure.

4. Remove the chicken from pressure cooker and transfer to a serving platter. Keep warm.

5. In a separate bowl, combine cornstarch with the water and whisk into the remaining liquid in the pressure cooker. Stir and boil over high heat for 3 minutes or until the sauce is thickened.

6. Pour sauce over chicken and serve.

Chicken Cacciatore

Serves 4

1 (3-pound) chicken, cut up

3 tablespoons all-purpose flour

1/2 teaspoon salt

1/8 teaspoon freshly ground black pepper

2 tablespoons vegetable or olive oil

1/4 cup diced salt pork

1 large onion, peeled and sliced

2 cloves garlic, peeled and minced

1 tablespoon dried parsley

2 teaspoons Mrs. Dash Italian Medley Seasoning Blend

2 large carrots, peeled and diced

1 stalk celery, diced

1 (15-ounce) can diced tomatoes

Salt and freshly ground black pepper, to taste

1/2 cup white wine

1 (6-ounce) can tomato paste

1. Trim and discard any extra fat from the chicken. Add the flour, salt, and pepper to a large zip-closure bag. Add the chicken, seal the bag, and shake to coat the chicken.

2. Bring the oil to temperature in the pressure cooker over medium-high heat. Add the salt pork and sauté until it begins to render its fat.

3. Add the meatier pieces of chicken, skin side down, and brown until crisp. Add the remaining ingredients except for the tomato paste.

4. Lock the lid into place. Bring to low pressure; maintain pressure for 20 minutes.

5. Remove the pan from the heat and quick-release the pressure. Place the chicken on a serving platter and keep warm.

6. Return the pan to the heat, stir the tomato paste into the sauce in pressure cooker, and simmer for 5 minutes or until thickened. Pour the sauce over chicken.

Turkey Thighs in Fig Sauce

Serves 4

4 (¾-pound) bone-in turkey thighs, skin removed

1 large onion, peeled and quartered

2 large carrots, peeled

½ stalk celery

½ cup balsamic vinegar

2 tablespoons tomato paste

1 cup chicken, turkey, or veal broth

Salt and freshly ground black pepper, to taste

12 dried figs, cut in half

Optional: Lemon zest, grated; ½ teaspoon chopped fresh rosemary

1. Add the turkey and onion to the pressure cooker. Cut the carrot and celery each into several pieces; add them. Add the balsamic vinegar, tomato paste, and broth to a bowl or measuring cup; whisk to combine and then pour into the pressure cooker. Season with the salt and pepper. Add the figs. Lock the lid into place and bring to high pressure; maintain pressure for 14 minutes. Remove from the heat and allow pressure to release naturally.

2. Remove the lid. Transfer the thighs, carrots, and figs to a serving platter. Tent loosely with aluminum foil and keep warm while you finish the sauce. Strain the pan juices. Discard the onion and celery. Skim and discard any fat. Pour the resulting strained sauce over the thighs. Serve.

Cranberry and Walnut Braised Turkey Wings

Serves 6

2 tablespoons butter

1 tablespoon vegetable oil

1 teaspoon salt

½ teaspoon black pepper

4 turkey wings (about 3 pounds)

1 onion, peeled and roughly sliced

1 cup dry cranberries (soaked in boiling water for 5 minutes)

1 cup shelled walnuts

1 bunch fresh thyme, tied with twine

1 cup freshly squeezed orange juice, or prepared juice without sugar

1. Heat butter and oil in an uncovered pressure cooker over medium heat. Sprinkle salt and pepper over turkey wings, and brown wings on both sides, making sure that the skin side is nicely colored.

2. Remove the wings from the pressure cooker and add the onion. Return wings to the pan, skin side up, along with cranberries, walnuts, and thyme. Pour the orange juice over the turkey. Close and lock the lid.

3. Turn the heat up to high. When the cooker reaches pressure, lower the heat to the minimum needed to maintain pressure. Cook for 12–15 minutes at high pressure.

4. Open with the natural release method—move the pressure cooker to a cool burner and wait for the pressure to come down on its own (about 10 minutes). For electric pressure cookers, disengage the "keep warm" mode or unplug the cooker. After 10 minutes, release the rest of the pressure using the valve.

5. Remove and discard the thyme bundle and carefully move the turkey wings to a serving dish. Tent with foil.

6. Reduce the contents of the liquid in the uncovered pressure cooker to about half. Pour the liquid, walnuts, onions, and cranberries over the wings and serve.

Duck in Orange Sauce

Serves 4

4 duck leg thigh sections

1 tablespoon duck fat or vegetable oil

1 stalk celery, diced

1 large carrot, peeled and grated

2 large shallots, peeled and minced

3 cloves garlic, peeled and minced

¼ cup triple sec or Grand Marnier

½ cup dry white wine

⅛ teaspoon dried thyme

1 teaspoon dried parsley

Optional: ⅛ teaspoon dried sage

Zest (divided) and juice of 1 orange

2 tablespoons white wine or sherry vinegar

Salt and freshly ground black pepper, to taste

1. Rinse the duck legs, blot dry, and place in the pressure cooker skin side down. Fry over medium-high heat for about 7 minutes on each side. Remove and keep warm.

2. Remove and discard all but 1 tablespoon of fat rendered from the duck. Reduce heat to medium and add the celery and carrots; sauté for 2 minutes. Add the shallots; sauté for 2 minutes or until they begin to soften. Stir in the garlic and sauté for 30 seconds.

3. Add the triple sec or Grand Marnier, white wine, thyme, parsley, and sage if using. Add ¼ of the orange zest. Return the browned duck legs to the pressure cooker. Lock the lid into place and bring to high pressure; maintain pressure for 45 minutes.

4. Quick-release the pressure, remove the lid, and transfer the duck legs to a serving platter; keep warm. Use an immersion blender to purée the vegetables and juices remaining in the pressure cooker. Stir in the remaining orange zest, orange juice, and half the vinegar. Taste for seasoning and add remaining vinegar if desired, and salt and pepper if needed. Pour the sauce over the duck legs. Serve.

Duck in Orange Sauce

Braised Turkey Breast with Cranberry Chutney

Serves 6

2 cups cranberry juice

1 cup whole cranberries

1 large sweet onion, peeled and diced

1 (3-pound) whole turkey breast

1 teaspoon dried thyme

Salt and freshly ground black pepper, to taste

2 tablespoons butter, melted

1 teaspoon orange zest, grated

1 tablespoon lemon juice

¼ cup light brown sugar

1. Place the rack in the pressure cooker. Add the cranberry juice, cranberries, and onion.

2. Rinse the turkey breast and pat dry with paper towels. Sprinkle the thyme, salt, and pepper over the breast. Place the turkey on the rack.

3. Lock the lid into place and bring to low pressure; maintain pressure for 25 minutes. Remove from the heat and allow pressure to release naturally.

4. Transfer the turkey breast to a broiling rack. Brush the skin with the melted butter. Place under the broiler; broil until the skin is browned and crisp.

5. Transfer the turkey to a serving platter and tent with aluminum foil; let rest for 10 minutes before carving.

6. Drain all but about ¼ cup of the juice from the cranberries and onions. Stir in the orange zest and lemon juice.

7. Return the pressure cooker to the heat and bring contents to a boil. Taste and stir in brown sugar to taste. Maintain a low boil until the mixture is thickened. Transfer to a serving bowl and serve with the turkey.

Turkey in Creamy Tarragon Sauce

Serves 4

4 slices bacon

1 pound skinless, boneless turkey breast

1 medium sweet onion, peeled and diced

2 cloves garlic, peeled and minced

½ cup dry white wine

2 tablespoons minced fresh tarragon

1 cup heavy cream

Salt and freshly ground black pepper, to taste

1. Cook the bacon in the pressure cooker over medium heat until crisp. Move the cooked bacon to paper towels and set aside.

2. Cut the turkey into bite-sized pieces and add to the pressure cooker along with the onion.

3. Stir-fry for 5 minutes or until the turkey is lightly browned and the onion is transparent. Stir in the garlic and sauté for 30 seconds. Deglaze the pan with the wine.

4. Lock the lid into place and bring to low pressure; maintain low pressure for 8 minutes. Remove from the heat and allow pressure to release naturally.

5. Remove the lid. Use a slotted spoon to transfer the cooked turkey to a serving bowl; keep warm.

6. Return the pressure cooker to medium heat. Stir the fresh tarragon into the pan juices. Bring the pan juices to a simmer. Whisk in the heavy cream; simmer until the cream is heated through.

7. Taste for seasoning and add salt and pepper if desired. Pour the sauce over the cooked turkey. Crumble the bacon over the top of the dish. Serve.

Turkey Breast in Yogurt Sauce

Serves 6

1 cup plain yogurt

1 teaspoon ground turmeric

1 teaspoon ground cumin

1 teaspoon yellow mustard seeds

¼ teaspoon salt

½ teaspoon freshly ground black pepper

1 pound boneless turkey breast

1 tablespoon ghee or butter

1 (1-pound) bag baby peas and pearl onions

1. In a bowl large enough to hold the turkey, mix together the yogurt, turmeric, cumin, mustard seeds, salt, and pepper.

2. Cut the turkey into bite-sized pieces. Stir into the yogurt mixture. Cover and marinate in the refrigerator for 4 hours.

3. Melt the ghee or butter in the pressure cooker. Add the turkey and yogurt mixture.

4. Lock the lid into place and bring to low pressure; maintain pressure for 8 minutes. Remove from the heat and let pressure release naturally for 5 minutes. Quick-release any remaining pressure.

5. Remove the lid and stir in the peas and pearl onions. Return pan to medium heat.

6. Simmer and stir until the vegetables are cooked through and the sauce is thickened. Serve immediately.

CHAPTER 8

Pork Entrées

Balsamic Pork Chops with Figs

Serves 4

4 (1"-thick) bone-in pork loin chops

Salt and freshly ground black pepper, to taste

2 teaspoons butter or ghee

2 teaspoons extra-virgin olive oil

2 medium sweet onions, peeled and sliced

4 cloves garlic, peeled and minced

$\frac{1}{2}$ teaspoon dried thyme

3 tablespoons balsamic vinegar

2 tablespoons dry white wine

$\frac{1}{2}$ cup chicken broth

10 ounces dried figs

1. Lightly season the pork chops on both sides by sprinkling them with salt and pepper. Add the butter or ghee and oil to the pressure cooker and bring to temperature over medium-high heat. Add 2 pork chops; brown for 3 minutes on each side. Move chops to a plate and repeat with the other 2 chops. Remove those chops to the plate.

2. Add the onions; sauté for 4 minutes or until the onions are transparent. Stir in the garlic; sauté for 30 seconds. Stir in the thyme and balsamic vinegar. Cook uncovered until the vinegar is reduced by half. Stir in the wine and broth. Add the pork chops, spooning some of the onions over the chops. Place the figs on top.

3. Lock the lid into place and bring to high pressure; maintain pressure for 9 minutes. Remove from the heat and quick-release the pressure. Serve immediately.

Rosemary Pork Shoulder with Apples

Serves 6

1 (3½-pound) pork shoulder roast

3 tablespoons Dijon mustard

1 tablespoon olive or vegetable oil

½ cup dry white wine, apple juice, or water

2 tart apples, peeled and quartered

3 cloves garlic, peeled and minced

Salt and freshly ground black pepper, to taste

1 teaspoon dried rosemary

1. Coat all sides of the roast with the mustard. Bring the oil to temperature in the pressure cooker over medium-high heat. Add the pork roast; brown the roast on all sides, reducing the heat if necessary to avoid burning the mustard.

2. Pour the wine, apple juice, or water around the roast. Working around the roast, use the liquid to deglaze the pan, scraping up any browned bits sticking to the bottom of the pan. Add the apples, garlic, salt, pepper, and rosemary.

3. Lock the lid into place and bring to low pressure; maintain pressure for 45 minutes. Remove from heat and allow pressure to release naturally.

4. Remove the lid. Use a meat thermometer to measure whether the roast has reached an internal temperature of 160°F.

5. Remove the roast to a serving platter. Tent and keep warm while you use an immersion blender to purée the pan contents. Slice the roast and pour the puréed juices over the slices. Serve.

Barbecue Western Ribs

Barbecue Western Ribs

Serves 4

1 cup barbecue sauce

½ cup apple jelly

1 (3") cinnamon stick

6 whole cloves

1 large sweet onion, peeled and diced

½ cup water

3 pounds pork Western ribs

1. Add the barbecue sauce, jelly, cinnamon stick, cloves, onion, and water to the pressure cooker. Stir to mix.

2. Add the ribs, ladling some of the sauce over them. Lock the lid into place and bring to low pressure; maintain pressure for 55 minutes. Remove from heat and allow pressure to release naturally.

3. Use a slotted spoon to remove the meat and bones; cover and keep warm. Skim any fat from the sauce in the cooker.

4. Remove and discard the cinnamon stick and cloves. Return the pressure cooker to medium-high heat.

5. Cook uncovered for 15 minutes or until the sauce is reduced and coats the back of a spoon. Either remove the meat from the bones and stir back into the sauce or pour the sauce into a gravy boat and pass at the table.

Ground Pork and Eggplant Casserole

Serves 8

2 pounds lean ground pork

1 large yellow onion, peeled and diced

1 stalk celery, diced

1 green pepper, seeded and diced

2 medium eggplants, diced into ½" pieces

4 cloves garlic, peeled and minced

⅛ teaspoon dried thyme, crushed

1 tablespoon freeze-dried parsley

3 tablespoons tomato paste

Optional: 1 teaspoon hot sauce

2 teaspoons Worcestershire sauce

Salt and freshly ground black pepper, to taste

1 large egg, beaten

½ cup chicken broth

1. Bring the pressure cooker to temperature over medium-high heat. Add the ground pork, onion, celery, and green pepper to the pressure cooker and stir-fry until the pork is no longer pink, breaking it apart as it cooks.

2. Drain and discard any fat rendered from the meat. Add the eggplant, garlic, thyme, parsley, tomato paste, hot sauce (if using), Worcestershire sauce, salt, pepper, and egg; stir to combine.

3. Pour in the chicken broth. Lock the lid into place and bring to low pressure; maintain pressure for 10 minutes. Remove from heat and allow pressure to release naturally.

Roast Pork with Cranberries and Sweet Potatoes

Serves 6

1 (3-pound) pork butt roast

Salt and freshly ground black pepper, to taste

1 (16-ounce) can sweetened whole cranberries

1 medium onion, peeled and diced

¼ cup orange marmalade

½ cup orange juice

¼ teaspoon ground cinnamon

⅛ teaspoon ground cloves

3 large sweet potatoes, peeled and quartered

Optional: 1 tablespoon cornstarch; 2 tablespoons cold water

1. Place the pork, fat side down, in the pressure cooker. Salt and pepper to taste. Combine the cranberries, onion, marmalade, orange juice, cinnamon, and cloves in a large measuring cup; stir to mix and then pour over the pork roast.

2. Arrange the sweet potatoes around the meat. Lock the lid into place and bring to low pressure; maintain pressure for 45 minutes. Remove from heat and allow pressure to release naturally.

3. To serve with a thickened sauce, transfer the meat and sweet potatoes to a serving platter. Cover and keep warm. Skim any fat off of the pan juices, making sure you have 2 cups of juice remaining in the cooker.

4. Return the pressure cooker to medium heat. Combine the cornstarch with the water. Whisk into the liquid in the pressure cooker; simmer and stir for 2 minutes, or when the cornstarch flavor has cooked out of the sauce and it is thickened and bubbly.

Swedish Meatballs

Serves 4

1 slice whole-wheat bread

½ cup milk

1 pound lean ground beef

8 ounces lean ground pork

1 large egg

1 small onion, peeled and minced

1 teaspoon dried dill

Salt and freshly ground black pepper, to taste

4 tablespoons butter

¼ cup all-purpose flour

1½ cups beef broth

1 cup water

½ cup heavy cream or sour cream

1. Add the bread to a large bowl. Pour in the milk and soak the bread until the milk is absorbed.

2. Break up the bread and mix it into the beef, pork, egg, onion, dill, salt, and pepper. Form into 12 meatballs and set aside.

3. Add the butter to the pressure cooker and melt it over medium-high heat; whisk in the flour until it forms a paste. Whisk in the broth and water. Bring to a simmer and then add the meatballs.

4. Lock the lid into place and bring to high pressure; maintain pressure for 10 minutes. Remove from the heat and quick-release the pressure.

5. Carefully stir in the cream. Taste for seasoning and add additional salt and pepper if needed. Serve.

Beer BBQ Pork Sliders with Apple

Serves 6

1½ pounds pork Western ribs

½ cup beer (your choice)

1 apple, peeled, cored, and roughly sliced

1 onion, peeled and diced

1 teaspoon raw sugar

1 teaspoon salt

½ teaspoon black pepper

12 whole-wheat slider buns, or 6 whole-wheat hamburger buns

1. Place ribs in the pressure cooker. Pour in beer and add the apple, onion, sugar, salt, and pepper. Close and lock the lid.

2. Turn the heat up to high. When the cooker reaches pressure, lower the heat to the minimum needed to maintain pressure. Cook for 15–20 minutes at high pressure.

3. Open with the natural release method—move the pressure cooker to a cool burner and wait for the pressure to come down on its own (about 10 minutes). For electric pressure cookers, disengage the "keep warm" mode or unplug the cooker and open when the pressure indicator has gone down (20–30 minutes).

4. Move the meat and bones to a cutting board using a slotted spoon. Remove and discard any fat still on the meat. Use two forks to shred the meat.

5. Skim and discard any fat from the top of the pan juices. Blend the contents of the pressure cooker using an immersion blender. Stir the shredded pork back into the cooker and simmer, uncovered, on medium heat for 5 minutes.

6. Spoon the meat onto hamburger buns and serve.

Sweet and Sour Pork

Serves 8

2 pounds pork shoulder

1 tablespoon all-purpose flour

2 tablespoons sesame or peanut oil

1 (14-ounce) can pineapple chunks

1 tablespoon light brown sugar

$\frac{1}{8}$ teaspoon mustard powder

$\frac{1}{2}$ teaspoon ground ginger

2 tablespoons apple cider vinegar

1 tablespoon liquid aminos or low-sodium soy sauce

4 medium carrots, peeled and sliced

1 large red bell pepper, seeded and sliced

$\frac{1}{2}$ pound fresh sugar snap peas

2 cups fresh broccoli florets

2 cloves garlic, peeled and thinly sliced

2 large sweet onions, peeled and diced, divided

2 tablespoons cornstarch

2 tablespoons cold water

1 cup bean sprouts

1. Cut the pork into bite-sized pieces. Add to a zip-closure bag along with the flour; seal and shake to coat the pork in the flour.

2. Bring the oil to temperature in the pressure cooker over medium-high heat. Fry the pork for 3 minutes or until it begins to brown. Add the pineapple juice and reserve the pineapple chunks; stir and scrape up any bits stuck to the bottom of the pan.

3. Add the sugar, mustard powder, ginger, vinegar, liquid aminos or soy sauce, carrots, red bell pepper, and sugar snap peas. Cut the broccoli florets into bite-sized pieces and add them to the pressure cooker. Add the garlic and $\frac{3}{4}$ of the diced onion. Lock the lid into place and bring to low pressure; maintain pressure for 12 minutes.

4. Quick-release the pressure. Use a slotted spoon to transfer all solids from the pressure cooker to a serving bowl; keep warm.

5. To make the glaze, in a small bowl mix together the cornstarch and water. Stir in some of the pan juices. Put the pressure cooker over medium heat. Bring to a boil and then whisk in the cornstarch mixture.

6. Reduce the heat to maintain a simmer for 3 minutes or until the mixture is thickened and the raw cornstarch taste is cooked out of the glaze. Stir in the bean sprouts, reserved pineapple chunks, and the remaining diced onion. Pour over the cooked pork and vegetables in the serving bowl; stir to combine. Serve.

Sweet and Sour Pork

Carnitas in Lettuce Cups

Serves 8

1 tablespoon unsweetened cocoa powder

1 tablespoon salt

1 teaspoon red pepper flakes

2 teaspoons oregano

1 teaspoon white pepper

1 teaspoon garlic powder

1 teaspoon cumin

1/8 teaspoon coriander

1/8 teaspoon cayenne pepper

1 large onion, peeled and finely chopped

4 pounds pork roast, leg, or shoulder

3 tablespoons vegetable oil, divided

Water for cooking

1 head butter lettuce, washed and dried

2 carrots, peeled and grated

2 limes, cut into wedges

1. The day before, make the rub spice mix. Combine cocoa powder, salt, red pepper flakes, oregano, white pepper, garlic powder, cumin, coriander, cayenne pepper, and onion. Cut the roast into manageable pieces and rub the pieces with the spice mixture. Wrap the meat in butcher's paper or foil and refrigerate overnight.

2. Heat 2 tablespoons oil in an uncovered pressure cooker over medium heat. Brown the roast on all sides. Add enough water to almost cover the meat (2–3 cups). Close and lock the lid.

3. Turn the heat up to high. When the cooker reaches pressure, lower the heat to the minimum needed to maintain pressure. Cook for 45–60 minutes at high pressure.

4. Open with the natural release method—move the pressure cooker to a cool burner and wait for the pressure to come down on its own (about 10 minutes). For electric pressure cookers, disengage the "keep warm" mode or unplug the cooker. After 10 minutes, release the rest of the pressure using the valve.

5. Remove the pork from the cooker and place on a platter. Using two forks, shred the meat into strips. Set aside.

6. In the meantime, reduce the cooking liquid in the cooker by half. Cool the liquid and remove the layer of fat that rises to the top.

Carnitas in Lettuce Cups—continued

7. In a large, wide sauté pan, heat 1 tablespoon oil and fry the shredded pork until it becomes lightly brown, about 5 minutes. Pour the cooking liquid over the pulled pork and heat through.

8. To make lettuce wraps, carefully remove the outer leaves of the lettuce and arrange on a platter with carrots. Fill with pork and finish with a squirt of fresh lime before serving.

Pork Roast with Root Beer Gravy

Serves 6

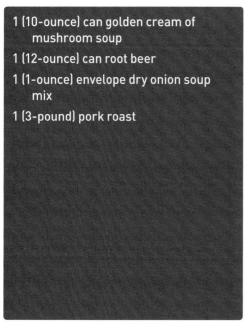

1 (10-ounce) can golden cream of mushroom soup

1 (12-ounce) can root beer

1 (1-ounce) envelope dry onion soup mix

1 (3-pound) pork roast

1. Add the soup, root beer, and onion soup mix to the pressure cooker. Stir to mix. Add the pork roast.

2. Lock the lid in place. Bring to low pressure; maintain pressure for 45 minutes. Remove from the heat and allow pressure to release naturally.

3. Transfer the roast to a serving platter; let rest for 5 minutes before slicing.

4. Skim any fat from the gravy in the pressure cooker. Stir to mix and then transfer to a gravy boat or pour over the sliced meat.

Sesame Pork with Pineapple

Serves 6

1 (14-ounce) can pineapple chunks

2 pounds pork shoulder

1 tablespoon all-purpose flour

2 tablespoons sesame oil

1 tablespoon raw sugar

1/8 teaspoon mustard powder

1/2 teaspoon ground ginger

2 tablespoons apple cider vinegar

1 tablespoon soy sauce

4 medium carrots, peeled and sliced

1 large red bell pepper, seeded and diced into 1" pieces

1/2 pound fresh sugar snap peas

1 1/2 cups fresh broccoli florets, cut into bite-sized pieces

2 cloves garlic, peeled and thinly sliced

1 large onion, peeled and sliced

2 tablespoons cornstarch

2 tablespoons cold water

1/4 cup bean sprouts

1 tablespoon sesame seeds

1. Drain pineapple, reserving juice. Set both aside.

2. Cut the pork into bite-sized pieces. Add to a zip-closure bag along with the flour. Seal bag and shake to coat the pork in the flour. Remove pork from bag with tongs and shake off excess flour (too much flour in the cooker could prevent it from reaching pressure).

3. Heat oil in an uncovered pressure cooker over medium heat. Sauté the pork for 3 minutes or until it begins to brown.

4. Deglaze the pan with the pineapple juice. Stir and scrape up any bits stuck to the bottom of the pan. Add the sugar, mustard powder, ginger, vinegar, soy sauce, carrots, red pepper, peas, broccoli, garlic, and onion. Close and lock the lid.

5. Turn the heat up to high. When the cooker reaches pressure, lower the heat to the minimum needed to maintain pressure. Cook for 18–20 minutes at high pressure.

6. When time is up, open the pressure cooker by quick-releasing the pressure.

7. Using a slotted spoon, move pork and vegetables to a serving bowl and keep warm using foil tent.

8. To make the glaze, mix together the cornstarch and water in a small bowl. Stir in a couple of tablespoons of the pan juices.

9. Put the uncovered pressure cooker over medium heat. Bring pan juices to a boil and whisk in the cornstarch mixture.

10. Reduce the heat to maintain a simmer for 3 minutes or until the mixture is thickened. Stir in the bean sprouts and reserved pineapple chunks. Pour over the cooked pork and vegetables in the serving bowl. Stir to combine.

11. Sprinkle with sesame seeds and serve.

Sausages with Sautéed Onions and Green Peppers

Serves 8

8 sausages

1 tablespoon olive oil

1 large green bell pepper, seeded and sliced

1 large red bell pepper, seeded and sliced

1 large orange bell pepper, seeded and sliced

1 large yellow bell pepper, seeded and sliced

2 large sweet onions, peeled and sliced

2 cloves garlic, peeled and minced

½ cup chicken broth

1. Add half of the sausages to the pressure cooker and brown them over medium-high heat. Remove them to a plate and brown the remaining sausages.

2. Drain and discard any rendered fat in the pressure cooker. Add the olive oil and bring it to temperature. Add the sliced peppers; sauté for 3 minutes or until they begin to get soft. Add the onion slices; sauté for 3 minutes or until the onions are transparent. Add the garlic; sauté for 30 seconds.

3. Return the sausages to the pressure cooker, pushing them down into the peppers and onions. Pour in the broth. Lock the lid into place and bring to high pressure; maintain pressure for 4 minutes. Quick-release the pressure. Serve.

Pork Steak in Fruit Sauce

Serves 6

8 pitted prunes

4 (8-ounce) pork steaks, trimmed of fat

2 small Granny Smith apples, peeled, cored, and sliced

½ cup dry white wine or apple juice

½ cup heavy cream

Salt and freshly ground black pepper, to taste

1 tablespoon red currant jelly

Optional: 1 tablespoon butter

1. Add the prunes, pork steaks, apple slices, wine or apple juice, and cream to the pressure cooker. Salt and pepper to taste.

2. Lock the lid into place and bring to high pressure; maintain pressure for 9 minutes. Quick-release the pressure.

3. Remove the meat and fruit to a serving platter. Either leave the pan juices as they are and keep them warm or skim the fat from the liquid in the pressure cooker and use an immersion blender to blend the fruit into the creamy broth.

4. Leave the pressure cooker on the heat and simmer uncovered for 10 minutes or until the mixture is reduced by half and thickened. Whisk in the red currant jelly. Taste for seasoning and add more salt and pepper if needed. Whisk in the butter a teaspoon at a time if you want a richer, glossier sauce. Ladle the sauce over the meat or pour it into a heated gravy boat.

Chinese Pork Ribs

Serves 6

¾ cup ketchup

½ cup water

¼ cup soy sauce

2 tablespoons balsamic or apple cider vinegar

⅓ cup light brown sugar

2 teaspoons ground ginger

1 teaspoon Chinese five-spice powder

1 teaspoon garlic powder

4 pounds baby back ribs

Optional: Lime wedges, for garnish; liquid smoke, to taste

1. Add the ketchup, water, soy sauce, vinegar, brown sugar, ginger, five-spice powder, and garlic powder to the pressure cooker; stir to combine.

2. Cut ribs into single ribs and add to the pressure cooker, submerging in the sauce.

3. Lock the lid into place and bring to low pressure; maintain pressure for 30 minutes. Remove from the heat and allow pressure to release naturally.

4. Transfer the ribs to a serving platter. If desired, garnish with lime wedges.

5. Remove and discard any fat from the sauce in the pressure cooker. Add up to 1 tablespoon of liquid smoke, to taste, if desired. If necessary, thicken the sauce by simmering it for several minutes over medium heat. Pour sauce into a gravy boat to pass at the table.

Jambalaya

Chapter 8: Pork Entrées

Jambalaya

Serves 6

2 tablespoons bacon fat or peanut oil

1 large carrot, peeled and grated

1 stalk celery, finely diced

1 large green bell pepper, seeded and chopped

1 medium yellow onion, peeled and diced

2 green onions, chopped

2 cloves garlic, peeled and minced

1/2 pound pork steak

1/2 pound boneless, skinless chicken thighs

1/2 pound smoked sausage, thinly sliced

1/2 pound cooked ham, diced

1 (15-ounce) can diced tomatoes, drained

2 cups chicken broth

1/2 tablespoon dried parsley

1/2 teaspoon dried thyme

1/4 teaspoon hot sauce, or to taste

2 tablespoons Worcestershire sauce

1/2 pound shrimp, peeled and deveined

Salt and freshly ground black pepper, to taste

6 servings cooked long-grain brown rice

1. Add the bacon fat or oil to the pressure cooker and bring it to temperature over medium heat.

2. Add the grated carrots, celery, and green bell pepper to the pan; sauté for 3–5 minutes or until soft. Add the yellow and green onions and sauté until transparent.

3. Add the garlic and sauté for an additional 30 seconds. Cut the pork and chicken into bite-sized pieces. Add to the pressure cooker and stir-fry for 3 minutes.

4. Stir in the smoked sausage and stir-fry for 3 minutes; add the ham and stir-fry for 1 minute.

5. Stir in the tomatoes, broth, parsley, thyme, hot sauce, and Worcestershire sauce. Lock the lid into place and bring to low pressure; maintain pressure for 8 minutes.

6. Quick-release the pressure. If the shrimp are large, halve them; otherwise, add the shrimp to the pot, cover, and cook over medium heat for 3–5 minutes or until shrimp are cooked.

7. Taste for seasoning and add salt and pepper if needed. Serve over the rice or stir the rice into the Jambalaya.

Apple Harvest Pork Western Ribs

Serves 12

3 pounds pork Western ribs

1 (12-ounce) can beer

1 cup unsweetened applesauce

1 large sweet onion, peeled and diced

2 tablespoons brown sugar

$\frac{1}{2}$ teaspoon freshly ground black pepper

Salt, to taste

Optional: Orange marmalade or apple jelly

12 hamburger buns

12 tablespoons coleslaw

1. Add the pork to the pressure cooker. Do not trim the fat from the ribs; it's what helps the meat cook up moist enough to shred for sandwiches. A lot of the fat will melt out of the meat as it cooks.

2. Pour the beer over the pork. Add the applesauce, onion, brown sugar, black pepper, and salt. Lock the lid into place and bring to low pressure; maintain pressure for 55 minutes. Remove from heat and allow pressure to release naturally.

3. Remove the lid and use a slotted spoon to move the pork to a cutting board. Remove and discard any fat still on the meat. Use two forks to shred the meat. Skim and discard any fat from the top of the pan juices. Stir the shredded pork back into the sauce. Place the pressure cooker over medium heat and bring to a simmer. Taste for seasoning; stir in orange marmalade or apple jelly a tablespoon at a time if you prefer a sweeter barbecue.

4. Spoon the meat onto hamburger buns. Top the meat with a heaping tablespoon of coleslaw.

Pork Loin Dinner

Serves 4

1 pound boneless pork loin

1 tablespoon vegetable oil

1 small onion, peeled and diced

Salt and freshly ground black pepper, to taste

½ cup white wine or apple juice

1 cup chicken broth

1 rutabaga, peeled and diced

1 large turnip, peeled and diced

4 small Yukon Gold or red potatoes, scrubbed

4 carrots, peeled and diced

1 stalk celery, finely diced

½ cup sliced leeks, white part only

½ teaspoon mild curry powder

¼ teaspoon dried thyme

2 teaspoons dried parsley

3 tablespoons fresh lemon juice

2 Granny Smith or tart green apples, peeled, cored, and diced

Optional: Fresh parsley or thyme sprigs

1. Cut the pork into 1" cubes. Add the oil to the pressure cooker and bring to temperature over medium heat. Add the onion; sauté for 3 minutes. Add the pork and lightly season it with salt and pepper. Stir-fry the pork for 5 minutes or until it just begins to brown. Add the wine or apple juice, broth, rutabaga, and turnip. Cut the potatoes into quarters and add them to the pot along with the carrots, celery, leeks, curry powder, thyme, parsley, and lemon juice.

2. Lock the lid into place and bring to high pressure; maintain pressure for 15 minutes. Turn off the heat and allow the pressure to drop naturally.

3. Carefully remove the lid and add the diced apples. Bring to a simmer over medium heat; reduce the heat and simmer covered for 5 minutes or until the apples are tender. Serve rustic style in large bowls, garnished with fresh parsley or thyme if desired.

Ham in Raisin Sauce

Serves 8

1 (4-pound) ready-to-eat ham
1 large sweet onion, peeled and sliced
1/8 teaspoon ground cloves
1/4 teaspoon ground ginger
1/2 teaspoon ground cinnamon
1 (14-ounce) can pineapple chunks
2 tablespoons brown sugar
1/2 cup raisins
1/2 cup apple butter
1/4 cup maple syrup
1 tablespoon balsamic vinegar

1. Add the ham and sliced onion to the pressure cooker. Stir together the cloves, ginger, cinnamon, pineapple juice (reserve the pineapple), brown sugar, and raisins. Pour over the ham.

2. Lock the lid into place. Bring to low pressure; maintain pressure for 20 minutes. Remove from the heat and allow pressure to release naturally.

3. Move the ham to a serving platter and keep warm while you finish the sauce.

4. Skim and remove any fat from the pan juices in the pressure cooker. Put the pan over medium heat; simmer to reduce the pan juices to about a cup. Stir in the pineapple chunks, apple butter, maple syrup, and vinegar. Taste for seasoning and adjust if necessary, adding additional maple syrup if you want a sweeter sauce or more vinegar if you need to cut the sweetness. Serve separately to spoon or pour over ham slices.

CHAPTER 9

Beef, Veal, and Lamb Entrées

Beef Braised in Beer

Serves 4

2 tablespoons Dijon mustard

Salt and freshly ground black pepper, to taste

1 teaspoon paprika

4 beef minute steaks, tenderized

1 tablespoon olive or vegetable oil

1 (12-ounce) bottle dark beer

2 tablespoons flour

1 tablespoon tomato paste

1 cup beef broth

1 medium yellow onion, peeled and diced

2 large carrots, peeled and diced

1 small stalk celery, finely diced

1 leek, white part only

1. Mix together the mustard, salt, pepper, and paprika. Spread both sides of the meat with the mustard mixture.

2. Bring the oil to temperature in the pressure cooker over medium-high heat. Fry the meat, 2 slices at a time, for 2 minutes on each side. Remove the meat and set aside.

3. Deglaze the pressure cooker with about ¼ cup of the beer, stirring and scraping to loosen any browned bits stuck to the bottom of the pan.

4. Whisk in the flour and the tomato paste. Whisk in the remaining beer. Add the beef back into the pan along with the broth, onion, carrots, and celery. Clean and slice the white part of the leek and add to the pressure cooker.

5. Lock the lid into place and bring to low pressure; maintain the pressure for 15 minutes. Remove from the heat and allow pressure to release naturally.

6. Remove the meat to a serving platter. If desired, use an immersion blender to purée the pan juices. Taste for seasoning and add additional salt and pepper if needed. Pour over the meat. Serve.

Citrus Corned Beef and Cabbage

Serves 6

Nonstick spray
2 medium onions, peeled and sliced
1 (3-pound) corned beef brisket
1 cup apple juice
¼ cup brown sugar, packed
2 teaspoons orange zest, finely grated
2 teaspoons prepared mustard
6 whole cloves
6 cabbage wedges

1. Treat the inside of the pressure cooker with nonstick spray. Arrange the onion slices across the bottom of the crock.

2. Trim and discard excess fat from the brisket and place it on top of the onions.

3. Add the apple juice, brown sugar, orange zest, mustard, and cloves to a bowl and stir to mix; pour over the brisket. Lock the lid into place and bring to low pressure; maintain for 45 minutes. Quick-release the pressure and remove the lid.

4. Place the cabbage on top of the brisket. Lock the lid into place and bring to low pressure; maintain pressure for 8 minutes. Quick-release the pressure and remove the lid.

5. Move the cabbage and meat to a serving platter, spooning some of the pan juices over the meat. Tent with aluminum foil and let rest for 15 minutes. Carve the brisket by slicing it against the grain. Remove and discard the cloves and any fat from the additional pan juices. Pour the pan juices into a gravy boat to pass at the table.

Hungarian Goulash

Serves 6

1 tablespoon olive or vegetable oil

1 green bell pepper, seeded and diced

4 large potatoes, peeled and diced

3 strips bacon, cut into 1" pieces

1 large yellow onion, peeled and diced

2 tablespoons sweet paprika

2½ pounds stewing beef or round steak

1 clove garlic, peeled and minced

Pinch caraway seeds, chopped

2 cups beef broth

1 (15-ounce) can diced tomatoes

2 tablespoons sour cream, plus more for serving

Salt and freshly ground black pepper, to taste

Optional: Spaetzle or egg noodles

1. Add the oil, bell pepper, potatoes, bacon, and onion to the pressure cooker over medium heat; sauté for 10 minutes or until the onion is transparent and the fat is rendering from the bacon.

2. Stir in paprika. Trim the beef of any fat and cut it into ½" cubes. Stir the beef into the vegetable mixture along with the garlic and caraway seeds.

3. Stir in the beef broth and tomatoes. Lock the lid into place and bring to low pressure; maintain pressure for 30 minutes.

4. Remove from heat and allow pressure to release naturally. Remove lid and stir 2 tablespoons sour cream into the goulash.

5. Taste for seasoning and add salt, pepper, and additional paprika if needed. Serve with additional sour cream on the side, and over prepared spaetzle or egg noodles if desired.

Hungarian Goulash

Chapter 9: Beef, Veal, and Lamb Entrées

Onion Steak

Serves 6

1 tablespoon olive or vegetable oil

4 large onions, peeled and sliced

1½ pounds round steak, cut into 6 pieces

4 cloves garlic, peeled and minced

1 tablespoon dried parsley

1 cup Beef Stock (see recipe in Chapter 4)

1 teaspoon dried thyme

½ teaspoon dried rosemary

Pinch dried red pepper flakes

Salt and freshly ground black pepper, to taste

¼ cup milk

2 tablespoons all-purpose flour

1. Use the oil to coat the bottom of the pressure cooker. In layers, add half of the onions, the meat, and the other half of the onions. Add the garlic, parsley, beef stock, thyme, rosemary, red pepper flakes, salt, and pepper. Lock the lid into place and bring to high pressure; maintain pressure for 14 minutes.

2. Quick-release the pressure and remove the lid. Move the meat to a serving platter; cover and keep warm. Whisk together the milk and flour, and then whisk the milk-flour paste into the onions and broth in the pan. Simmer and stir for 3 minutes or until the onion gravy is thickened and the flour taste is cooked out of the sauce. Pour over the meat or transfer to a gravy boat to pass at the table. Serve.

Barbecue Pot Roast

Serves 8

½ cup ketchup

½ cup apricot preserves

¼ cup dark brown sugar

¼ cup apple cider or white vinegar

½ cup teriyaki or soy sauce

Dry red pepper flakes, crushed, to taste

1 teaspoon dry mustard

¼ teaspoon freshly ground black pepper

1 (4-pound) boneless chuck roast

1½ cups water for beef

1 large sweet onion, peeled and sliced

1. Add the ketchup, preserves, brown sugar, vinegar, teriyaki or soy sauce, red pepper flakes, mustard, and pepper to a gallon-sized plastic freezer bag; close and squeeze to mix. Trim the roast of any fat, cut the meat into 1" cubes, and add to the bag. Refrigerate overnight.

2. Add the appropriate amount of water and the cooking rack or steamer basket to a 6-quart or larger pressure cooker. Place half of the sliced onions on the rack or basket. Use a slotted spoon to remove the roast pieces from the sauce and place them on the onions; reserve the sauce. Cover the roast pieces with the remaining onions.

3. Lock the lid in place on the pressure cooker. Place over medium heat and bring to high pressure; maintain for 50 minutes, or 15 minutes per pound. (Remember: You reduce the weight of the roast when you trim off the fat.) Turn off the heat and allow 15 minutes for the pressure to release naturally. Quick-release any remaining pressure, and then carefully remove the lid. Strain the meat (reserve the pan juices), separate it from the onions, and return it to the pan. Purée the onions in a food processor or blender.

4. Pour the reserved sauce into the cooker and use two forks to pull the meat apart and mix it into the sauce. Bring to a simmer over medium heat. Stir in the onion. Skim the sauce for fat. Add ½ cup of the pan juices to the cooker and stir into the meat and sauce. Reduce the heat to low and simmer for 15 minutes, or until the mixture is thick enough to serve on sandwiches.

Barbecued Beef

Serves 8

1 (3-pound) beef English roast
1 cup water
1/2 cup red wine
1/2 cup ketchup
1 tablespoon red wine vinegar
2 teaspoons Worcestershire sauce
2 teaspoons mustard powder
2 tablespoons dried minced onion
1 teaspoon dried minced garlic
1 teaspoon cracked black pepper
1 tablespoon brown sugar
1 teaspoon chili powder
1/2 teaspoon ground cinnamon
1/4 teaspoon ground cloves
1/4 teaspoon ground ginger
Pinch ground allspice
Pinch dried pepper flakes, crushed

1. Halve the roast and stack the halves in the pressure cooker. Mix together all the remaining ingredients and pour over the beef.

2. Lock the lid into place and bring to low pressure; maintain pressure for 55 minutes. Remove from the heat and allow pressure to release naturally.

3. Use a slotted spoon to remove the beef from the pressure cooker; pull it apart, discarding any fat or gristle. Taste the meat and sauce and adjust seasonings if necessary.

4. To thicken the sauce, return the pressure cooker to the heat. Skim any fat off the surface of the sauce and simmer uncovered while you pull apart the beef. Stir occasionally to prevent the sauce from burning.

Swiss Steak Meal

Serves 6

2½ pounds beef round steak, 1" thick

1 tablespoon vegetable oil

Salt and freshly ground black pepper, to taste

1 medium yellow onion, peeled and diced

2 stalks celery, diced

1 large green pepper, seeded and diced

1 cup tomato juice

1 cup beef broth or water

6 large carrots, peeled

6 medium white potatoes, scrubbed

Optional: 4 teaspoons butter

1. Cut the round steak into 6 serving-sized pieces. Add the oil and bring it to temperature over medium heat. Season the meat on both sides with salt and pepper.

2. Add 3 pieces of the meat and fry for 3 minutes on each side to brown them. Move to a platter and repeat with the other 3 pieces of meat.

3. Leave the last 3 pieces of browned meat in the cooker; add the onion, celery, and green pepper on top of them. Lay in the other 3 pieces of meat and pour the tomato juice and broth or water over them. Place the carrots and potatoes on top of the meat.

4. Lock the lid into place; bring to high pressure and maintain the pressure for 17 minutes. Remove from the heat and allow pressure to release naturally.

5. Once pressure has dropped, open the cooker and move the potatoes, carrots, and meat to a serving platter. Cover and keep warm.

6. Skim any fat from the juices remaining in the pan. Set the uncovered cooker over medium heat and simmer the juices for 5 minutes.

7. Whisk in the butter, 1 teaspoon at a time, if desired. Taste for seasoning and add additional salt and pepper if needed.

8. Have the resulting gravy available at the table to pour over the meat. Serve immediately.

Beef Bourguignon

Chapter 9: Beef, Veal, and Lamb Entrées

Beef Bourguignon

Serves 8

8 slices bacon, diced

1 (3-pound) boneless English or chuck roast

Salt and freshly ground black pepper, to taste

1 large yellow onion, peeled and diced

2 tablespoons tomato paste

3 cloves garlic, peeled and minced

½ teaspoon dried thyme

1 bay leaf

4 cups Burgundy

1 large yellow onion, peeled and thinly sliced

½ cup plus 2 tablespoons butter, divided

16 ounces fresh mushrooms, sliced

2 cups beef broth or water

½ cup all-purpose flour

1. Add the bacon to the pressure cooker and fry over medium heat until it renders its fat; remove bacon and reserve for another use. Trim the roast of fat and cut into bite-sized pieces; add the beef pieces to the pressure cooker, sprinkle with salt and pepper to taste, and stir-fry for 5 minutes. Add the diced onion and sauté for 3 minutes or until the onion is tender. Add the tomato paste, garlic, and thyme; stir to coat the meat. Add the bay leaf and stir in enough of the Burgundy to cover the meat in the pan completely, being careful not to exceed the fill line in the pressure cooker. Lock the lid into place and bring to low pressure; maintain pressure for 45 minutes. Remove from heat and allow pressure to release naturally.

2. Add the sliced onion to a microwave-safe bowl along with 2 tablespoons of the butter; cover and microwave on high for 2 minutes. Add the mushrooms; cover and microwave on high for 1 minute. Stir, cover, and microwave on high in 30-second increments until the mushrooms are sautéed and the onion is transparent.

3. Quick-release any remaining pressure in the pressure cooker and remove the lid. Stir the mushroom-onion mixture into the pan. Lock the lid into place and bring to low pressure; maintain pressure for 5 minutes.

4. Quick-release the pressure and remove the lid. Stir in any remaining Burgundy and the broth or water. Increase the heat to medium-high and bring the contents of the pan to a boil.

5. In a small bowl or measuring cup, mix the remaining ½ cup of butter together with the flour to form a paste; whisk in some of the pan liquid a little at a time to thin the paste. Strain out any lumps if necessary.

6. Once the contents of the pressure cooker reach a boil, whisk the butter-flour mixture into the meat and juices in the pan; boil for 1 minute. Reduce the heat and simmer uncovered, cooking and stirring for 5 minutes or until the pan juices have been reduced and a gravy results.

Moroccan Lamb Tagine

Serves 6

1 teaspoon cinnamon powder

1 teaspoon ginger powder

1 teaspoon turmeric powder

1 teaspoon cumin powder

2 cloves garlic, peeled and crushed

3 tablespoons olive oil, divided

1 (3-pound) lamb shoulder, cut into 1" pieces

10 ounces dried plums

2 onions, peeled and roughly sliced

1 cup Vegetable Stock (see recipe in Chapter 4)

1 bay leaf

1 (3") cinnamon stick

3 tablespoons honey

1 teaspoon salt

1 teaspoon black pepper

½ cup sliced almonds, toasted

1 tablespoon sesame seeds

1. Mix the cinnamon powder, ginger, turmeric, cumin, and garlic with 2 tablespoons of olive oil to make a paste. Cover the lamb with this paste and set aside. Place the dried plums in a bowl and cover with boiling water. Set aside.

2. Heat 1 tablespoon olive oil in an uncovered pressure cooker over medium heat. Add onions and cook until softened (about 5 minutes). Remove onions and set aside.

3. Add the meat and brown on all sides (about 10 minutes). Deglaze the pressure cooker with the stock, scraping the bottom well and incorporating any browned bits into the rest of the sauce. Return onions to the pan and add the bay leaf and cinnamon stick. Close and lock the lid.

4. Turn the heat up to high. When the cooker reaches pressure, lower the heat to the minimum needed to maintain pressure. Cook for 25 minutes at high pressure.

5. Open with the natural release method—move the pressure cooker to a cool burner and wait for the pressure to come down on its own (about 10 minutes). For electric pressure cookers, disengage the "keep warm" mode or unplug the cooker and open when the pressure indicator has gone down (20–30 minutes).

6. Remove and discard the bay leaf and cinnamon stick. Return the pressure cooker to medium heat, then add honey, salt, pepper, and drained dried plums. Simmer, uncovered, until the liquid is reduced (about 5 minutes).

7. Sprinkle with toasted almonds and sesame seeds and serve.

Stuffed Head of Cabbage

Serves 6

1 pound lean ground beef

¼ cup butter

2 large sweet onions, peeled and diced

4 cloves garlic, peeled and minced

1 tablespoon dried parsley

2 tablespoons dried dill

1 teaspoon dried thyme

1 large carrot, peeled and diced

2 stalks celery, diced

1 cup long-grain white rice

2 cups beef or chicken broth, divided

2 (14-ounce) cans diced tomatoes, divided

1 teaspoon sugar

2 teaspoons salt, divided

1 teaspoon freshly ground black pepper, divided

1 large head green cabbage

¼ cup olive oil

1 small sweet onion, peeled and sliced

1 small green pepper, seeded and diced

1 tablespoon light brown sugar

2 teaspoons dried oregano

1. Add the ground beef to the pressure cooker. Fry it until cooked through over medium-high heat, breaking it apart as you do so. Drain and discard rendered fat. Transfer the cooked ground beef to a bowl and keep warm.

2. Reduce heat to medium. Melt the butter in the pressure cooker and bring it to temperature.

3. Add the 2 large diced onions; sauté for 3 minutes or until they begins to soften. Add the garlic; sauté for 30 seconds.

4. Mix in the parsley, dill, thyme, carrot, celery, rice, cooked ground beef, 1 cup of the broth, 1 can of the undrained tomatoes, sugar, 1 teaspoon of the salt, and ½ teaspoon of the pepper.

5. Lock the lid into place and bring to high pressure; maintain pressure for 6 minutes.

6. Remove the pressure cooker from heat, quick-release the pressure, and remove the lid. Stir and mix the ground beef–rice mixture.

7. Wash and dry the cabbage. Remove the outer leaves and the core. Use a paring knife to hollow out the cabbage, leaving at least a 2"-thick shell.

8. Center the cabbage shell on a 24" length of cheesecloth. Spoon the ground beef–rice mixture into the cabbage shell, mounding it over the top of the opening. Pull the cheesecloth up and over the top of the cabbage.

Stuffed Head of Cabbage—continued

9. Add the olive oil to the pressure cooker and bring it to temperature over medium heat.

10. Add the sliced onion and diced green pepper; sauté for 3 minutes or until the onion is soft.

11. Stir in brown sugar, oregano, remaining tomatoes, remaining broth, and remaining salt and pepper. Stir well. Place the steamer basket in the sauce in the pressure cooker.

12. Lift the cabbage by the ends of the cheesecloth and place it in the steamer basket.

13. Lock the lid into place and bring to high pressure; maintain pressure for 10 minutes. Remove the pressure cooker from the heat, quick-release the pressure, and remove the lid.

14. Transfer the cabbage to a serving platter by using tongs to hold the ends of the cheesecloth and a spatula to steady the bottom of the cabbage.

15. Carefully pull the cheesecloth out from the under the cabbage. Cut the cabbage into serving wedges.

16. Remove the steamer basket from the pressure cooker and pour the sauce over the cabbage wedges. Serve.

South African Ground Beef Casserole

Serves 8

1 cup 1% milk

2 slices stale white bread, torn in small pieces

2 tablespoons peanut oil

2 onions, peeled and chopped

1 tablespoon curry powder

¾ teaspoon turmeric

1 teaspoon salt

¼ teaspoon black pepper

2 pounds ground beef

2 tablespoons raw sugar

Zest and juice of 1 lemon

¼ cup sliced almonds, toasted

½ cup raisins, soaked and drained

1 tablespoon butter

1 cup water

5 eggs

4 bay leaves

1. In a bowl, pour milk over bread and set aside.

2. In a large, wide sauté pan over medium heat, heat the peanut oil. Add onions and sauté until soft (about 5 minutes). Add the curry powder, turmeric, salt, and pepper.

3. Add ground beef to pan and cook, stirring to crumble, until beef is browned and all of the liquid has evaporated (about 5–7 minutes). Turn off the heat and mix in the sugar.

4. Squeeze the bread and add it to the pan (keep the milk to use later for the topping). Add the lemon juice and zest, almonds, and raisins. Mix well.

5. Butter a 7½"-wide (or smaller) heatproof baking dish. Pour mixture into buttered baking dish and flatten slightly.

6. Prepare the pressure cooker by inserting the trivet, or steamer basket, and filling it with 1 cup of water. Make a foil sling by folding a long piece of foil into three and lower the uncovered dish into the pressure cooker. Close and lock the lid.

7. Turn the heat up to high. When the cooker reaches pressure, lower the heat to the minimum needed to maintain pressure. Cook for 15–20 minutes at high pressure.

8. When time is up, open the pressure cooker by quick-releasing the pressure.

9. Mix the eggs into the milk to make a custard mixture.

10. Carefully remove the baking dish from the pressure cooker and pour the custard mixture over the meat. Add the bay leaves and cover with foil. Lower dish into the pressure cooker again. Close and lock the lid.

11. Turn the heat up to high. When the cooker reaches pressure, lower the heat to the minimum needed to maintain pressure. Cook for 3–5 minutes at high pressure.

12. When time is up, open the pressure cooker by quick-releasing the pressure.

13. Serve as is or brown the custard under the broiler for about 5 minutes.

Greek Meatballs in Tomato Sauce

Serves 8

1½ pounds lean ground beef or lamb

1 cup uncooked rice

1 small yellow onion, peeled and finely chopped

3 cloves garlic, peeled and minced

2 teaspoons dried parsley

½ tablespoon dried oregano

1 large egg

All-purpose flour

2 cups tomato juice or tomato-vegetable juice

1 (14-ounce) can diced tomatoes

Optional: Water

2 tablespoons extra-virgin olive oil

Salt and freshly ground black pepper, to taste

1. Make the meatballs by mixing the ground beef or lamb together with the rice, onion, garlic, parsley, oregano, and egg; shape into small meatballs and roll each one in flour.

2. Add the tomato or tomato-vegetable juice and can of diced tomatoes to the pressure cooker. Carefully add the meatballs. If necessary, pour in enough water to completely cover the meatballs, making sure not to take the liquid above the fill line. Add the oil.

3. Lock the lid into place and bring to low pressure; maintain pressure for 10 minutes. Remove from heat and allow pressure to release naturally for 10 minutes. Quick-release any remaining pressure and remove the lid. Taste for seasoning and add salt and pepper if needed.

Beef Biryani

Serves 6

1 tablespoon ghee

1 onion, peeled and sliced

1 pound top round, cut into strips

1 tablespoon minced fresh ginger

2 cloves garlic, peeled and minced

1/2 teaspoon ground cloves

1/2 teaspoon ground cardamom

1/2 teaspoon ground coriander

1/2 teaspoon freshly ground black pepper

1/2 teaspoon cinnamon

1/2 teaspoon cumin

1 teaspoon salt

1 cup whole-milk plain yogurt

1 (28-ounce) can of whole stewed tomatoes

2 cups cooked basmati rice

1. Heat ghee in an uncovered pressure cooker over medium heat. Add onion and sauté until softened (about 5 minutes). Add the rest of the ingredients, except for the rice, to the pressure cooker.

2. Turn the heat up to high. When the cooker reaches pressure, lower the heat to the minimum needed to maintain pressure. Cook for 13–15 minutes at high pressure.

3. When time is up, open the pressure cooker by quick-releasing the pressure.

4. Simmer uncovered until most of the liquid has evaporated (about 10 minutes).

5. Serve over cooked basmati rice.

Mushroom-Stuffed Veal Roll

Serves 8

½ tablespoon unsalted butter

2 tablespoons olive oil, divided

8 ounces fresh button mushrooms, cleaned and sliced

4 ounces fresh shiitake mushrooms, cleaned and sliced

2 large shallots, peeled and minced

2 cloves garlic, peeled and minced, divided

1½ teaspoons salt, divided

3 tablespoons all-purpose flour

½ teaspoon freshly ground black pepper

1 (3½-pound) boneless veal shoulder roast, butterflied

4 ounces prosciutto, thinly sliced

1 large carrot, peeled and grated

1 stalk celery, finely diced

1 small onion, peeled and diced

1 cup dry white wine

1 cup veal or chicken broth

1. Heat butter and 1 tablespoon olive oil in an uncovered pressure cooker over medium heat. Sauté mushrooms for 3 minutes or until they begin to soften. Stir in the shallots, 1 clove garlic, and 1 teaspoon salt. Sauté for another 10 minutes or until the mushrooms have given off most of their moisture.

2. Add flour, ½ teaspoon salt, and pepper to a bowl. Stir to mix and set aside.

3. Place the veal roast cut side up on a flat working surface. Arrange the prosciutto over the cut side of the roast, overlapping the edges opposite the center of the roast by several inches. Spread all but ¼ cup of the sautéed mushroom mixture over the prosciutto up to where the prosciutto overlaps the edges of the roast. Fold the overlapped edges over the mushroom mixture and then roll the prosciutto-mushroom layers to the center of the roast. Pull the edges of the roast up and over the prosciutto-mushroom roll and secure at 1" intervals with butcher's twine.

4. Heat the remaining oil in the pressure cooker over medium-high heat. Add the roast and brown it for about 5 minutes on each side.

5. Remove roast from the cooker and add the carrot, celery, onion, and remaining clove of garlic to the pressure cooker and sauté for 5 minutes.

6. Deglaze the cooker with the wine and broth, and add the roast on top of the sautéed vegetables. Close and lock the lid.

7. Turn the heat up to high. When the cooker reaches pressure, lower the heat to the minimum needed to maintain pressure. Cook for 25–30 minutes (depending on the thickness) at high pressure.

8. Open with the natural release method—move the pressure cooker to a cool burner and wait for the pressure to come down on its own (about 10 minutes). For electric pressure cookers, disengage the "keep warm" mode or unplug the cooker and open when the pressure indicator has gone down (20–30 minutes).

9. Transfer the roast to a serving platter and tent loosely with aluminum foil. Let rest for at least 10 minutes before slicing.

10. Use an immersion blender to purée the pan juices and vegetables in the pressure cooker.

11. Slice the roast into ½" slices and either pour the thickened pan juices over the slices or serve with the sauce on the side.

Mediterranean Braised Lamb Shanks

Serves 4

¼ cup all-purpose flour

¼ teaspoon sea salt

¼ teaspoon freshly ground black pepper

4 (¾-pound) lamb shanks

1 tablespoon olive oil

1 large carrot, peeled and diced

1 medium onion, peeled and diced

2 cloves garlic, peeled and minced

1 tablespoon herbes de Provence

1 (14-ounce) can diced tomatoes

½ cup dry white wine

½ cup veal or chicken broth

1 bay leaf

1 (12-ounce) jar pimiento-stuffed olives, drained

1 (8-ounce) package frozen artichokes, thawed

1. Add the flour, salt, and pepper to a large zip-closure plastic bag. Shake to mix. Add the lamb shanks to the bag, seal the bag, and shake to coat them in the flour. Bring the oil to temperature in the pressure cooker over medium-high heat.

2. Remove 2 lamb shanks from the bag, shaking off any excess flour, and add them to the pressure cooker. Fry for about 10 minutes, turning them until they're browned on all sides. Transfer the browned lamb shanks from the pressure cooker to a platter and keep warm. Repeat with the remaining 2 lamb shanks.

3. Add the carrot to the oil in the pressure cooker; sauté for 1 minute. Add the onion and sauté for 3 minutes or until the onion begins to soften. Stir in the garlic; sauté for 30 seconds. Stir in the herbes de Provence, undrained tomatoes, wine, broth, and bay leaf.

4. Return the lamb shanks and their accumulated juices to the pressure cooker. Lock the lid in place and bring to high pressure; maintain pressure for 25 minutes. Remove from heat and allow pressure to release naturally for 10 minutes. Quick-release any remaining pressure and remove the lid.

5. Transfer the lamb shanks to an ovenproof platter and tent loosely with aluminum foil. Place in a warm (200°F) oven.

6. Place the pressure cooker over medium heat and bring the pan juices to a simmer. Stir in the olives and artichokes. Simmer, stirring occasionally, for 15 minutes or until the vegetables are heated through and the sauce is thickened.

7. Taste the sauce for seasoning and add salt and pepper if needed. Remove the platter with the lamb shanks from the oven, remove the foil, and pour the sauce over the lamb shanks. Serve.

Mock Enchiladas

Serves 8

2 pounds lean ground beef

1 large onion, peeled and diced

1 (4½-ounce) can chopped chilies

1 (12-ounce) jar mild enchilada sauce

1 (10½-ounce) can golden mushroom soup

1 (10½-ounce) can Cheddar cheese soup

1 (10½-ounce) can cream of mushroom soup

1 (10½-ounce) can cream of celery soup

2 cups refried beans

Plain corn tortilla chips, to taste

1. Add the ground beef and diced onion to the pressure cooker. Bring to high pressure and maintain for 5 minutes. Quick-release the pressure and remove the lid. Remove and discard any rendered fat. Stir the ground beef into the onions, breaking the beef apart.

2. Stir in the chilies, enchilada sauce, soups, and refried beans. Lock the lid into place and bring to low pressure; maintain pressure for 5 minutes. If you'll be serving the dish immediately, you can quick-release the pressure. Otherwise, remove from the heat and allow the pressure to release naturally.

3. Stir 8 ounces or more tortilla chips into the mixture in the pressure cooker. Cover and stir over medium-low heat for 15 minutes or until the tortilla chips are soft.

Steak Fajitas

Serves 4

1 pound round steak

1 small onion, peeled and diced

1 small green bell pepper, seeded and diced

Salt and freshly ground black pepper, to taste

2 cups frozen whole kernel corn, thawed

1¼ cups tomato juice

½ teaspoon chili powder

Optional: 1 tablespoon cornstarch; ¼ cup cold water

1. Trim and discard any fat from the meat. Cut the meat into ½" pieces and add to the pressure cooker. Stir in the onion, bell pepper, salt, pepper, corn, tomato juice, and chili powder. Lock the lid into place and bring to low pressure; maintain pressure for 12 minutes. Remove from the heat and allow pressure to release naturally for 5 minutes. Quick-release any remaining pressure.

2. Optional: To thicken the sauce, in a small bowl or measuring cup whisk the cornstarch together with the cold water. Return the pressure cooker to medium heat and bring to a simmer; whisk in the cornstarch slurry and cook uncovered for 5 minutes or until the sauce is thickened and the raw cornstarch taste is cooked out of the sauce. Taste for seasoning and add additional salt and pepper if needed.

CHAPTER 10

Fish and Seafood Entrées

Miso Red Snapper

Serves 4

Water

1 tablespoon red miso paste

1 tablespoon rice wine

2 teaspoons fermented black beans

2 teaspoons sesame oil

1 teaspoon dark soy sauce

½ teaspoon Asian chili paste

Salt

2 pounds red snapper fillets

1 (2") piece fresh ginger

2 cloves garlic, peeled and minced

4 green onions

1. Insert the rack in the pressure cooker. Pour in enough water to fill the pan to just below the top of the rack.

2. In a small bowl, mix the miso, rice wine, black beans, sesame oil, soy sauce, and chili paste. Lightly sprinkle salt over the fish fillets and then rub them on both sides with the miso mixture.

3. Peel the ginger and cut into matchsticks 1" long. Place half of them on the bottom of a glass pie plate. Sprinkle half the minced garlic over the ginger.

4. Halve the green onions lengthwise and then cut them into 2"-long pieces; place half of them over the ginger and garlic. Place the fish fillets in the pie plate and sprinkle the remaining ginger, garlic, and onions over the top. Place the pie plate on the rack inside the pressure cooker.

5. Lock the lid into place and bring to high pressure; maintain pressure for 3 minutes. Remove from heat and quick-release the pressure. Serve.

Fish en Papillote

Serves 6

3 pounds whitefish

6 tablespoons butter, softened

¼ cup fresh lemon juice

3 shallots, peeled and minced

2 cloves garlic, peeled and minced

1 tablespoon dried parsley

¼ teaspoon freshly ground white pepper

3 medium potatoes, peeled and cut into matchsticks

3 large carrots, peeled and cut into matchsticks

2 small zucchini, thinly sliced

Salt

Water

1. Thoroughly rinse the fish. Cut away and discard any grayish bands of fat. Cut into 6 portions.

2. In a small bowl, mix together the butter, lemon juice, shallots, garlic, parsley, and white pepper.

3. Cut out 6 pieces of parchment paper to wrap around the fish fillets. Brush the parchment with some of the butter mixture. Lay a fish fillet on each piece of parchment. Equally divide the remaining butter mixture among the fish, brushing it over the tops of the fillets.

4. Layer the potatoes, carrots, and zucchini on top of the fish. Salt each fillet-vegetable packet to taste. Enclose the fish and vegetables in the parchment by wrapping the paper envelope-style over them. Crisscross the packets in the steamer basket for your pressure cooker.

5. Add enough water to the pressure cooker to come up to the bottom of the steamer basket. Lock the lid into place and bring to high pressure; maintain pressure for 5 minutes. Remove from the heat and quick-release the pressure.

6. Remove the steamer basket from the pressure cooker. Using a spatula and tongs, transfer the packets to 6 serving plates. Serve immediately.

Catfish in Creole Sauce

Serves 4

1½ pounds catfish fillets

1 (15-ounce) can diced tomatoes

2 teaspoons dried minced onion

¼ teaspoon onion powder

1 teaspoon dried minced garlic

¼ teaspoon garlic powder

1 teaspoon hot paprika

¼ teaspoon dried tarragon

1 medium green bell pepper, seeded and diced

1 stalk celery, finely diced

¼ teaspoon sugar

½ cup chili sauce

Salt and freshly ground black pepper, to taste

1. Rinse the catfish in cold water and pat dry between paper towels. Cut into bite-sized pieces.

2. Add all ingredients except fish to the pressure cooker and stir to mix. Gently stir the fillets into the tomato mixture.

3. Lock the lid into place and bring the pressure cooker to low pressure; maintain pressure for 5 minutes. Quick-release the pressure. Remove the lid. Gently stir and then taste for seasoning. Add salt and pepper to taste if needed. Serve.

Tomato-Braised Calamari

Serves 6

3 tablespoons olive oil, divided

1 clove garlic, peeled and smashed

⅛ teaspoon hot pepper flakes

2 anchovies

1½ pounds fresh or frozen calamari, cleaned

½ cup white wine

1 (14½-ounce) can diced tomatoes

1 cup water

1 bunch parsley, chopped, divided

1 teaspoon salt

¼ teaspoon black pepper

1. Heat 2 tablespoons olive oil in an uncovered pressure cooker over low heat. Add the garlic clove, pepper flakes, and anchovies. Cook for 3 minutes, stirring constantly, to flavor the oil.

2. Add the calamari and sauté until lightly colored (about 5 minutes). Add the wine and let it evaporate a bit (about 3 minutes). Finally, add the tomatoes, water, and half the parsley. Close and lock the lid.

3. Turn the heat up to high. When the cooker reaches pressure, lower the heat to the minimum needed to maintain pressure. Cook for 15–20 minutes at high pressure.

4. When time is up, open the pressure cooker by quick-releasing the pressure.

5. Season with salt and pepper and sprinkle with remaining olive oil and parsley before serving.

Trout in Parsley Sauce

Serves 4

4 fresh 1/2-pound river trout

Salt, to taste

4 cups torn lettuce leaves

1 teaspoon distilled white or white wine vinegar

1/2 cup water

1/2 cup minced fresh flat-leaf parsley

1 shallot, peeled and minced

2 tablespoons mayonnaise

1/2 teaspoon fresh lemon juice

1/4 teaspoon sugar

Pinch salt

2 tablespoons sliced almonds, toasted

1. Rinse the trout inside and out; pat dry. Sprinkle with salt inside and out. Put 3 cups of the lettuce leaves in the bottom of the pressure cooker. Arrange the trout over the top of the lettuce and top the trout with the remaining lettuce. Stir the vinegar into the water and pour into the pressure cooker.

2. Lock the lid into place and bring to high pressure; maintain pressure for 3 minutes. Remove from the heat and allow pressure to release naturally for 3 minutes. Quick-release any remaining pressure.

3. Remove the lid and use a spatula to move the fish to a serving plate. Peel and discard the skin from the fish. Remove and discard the heads if desired.

4. To make the parsley sauce, mix together the parsley, shallot, mayonnaise, lemon juice, sugar, and salt. Evenly divide among the fish, spreading it over them. Sprinkle the toasted almonds over the top of the sauce. Serve.

Vietnamese-Style Seafood Stew

Serves 4

2 cloves garlic, peeled and minced

1 small apple, peeled, cored, and diced

1 banana, peeled and sliced

½ cup raisins

2 tablespoons light brown sugar

¼ teaspoon ground cumin

¼ teaspoon saffron

2 tablespoons curry powder

2 cups chicken broth

2 cups unsweetened coconut milk

2 tablespoons lemon or lime juice

1 teaspoon Worcestershire sauce

¾ cup heavy cream

32 shrimp, peeled and deveined

16 sea scallops

1 pound cod, halibut, snapper, or other firm white fish

1 small red bell pepper, seeded and diced

½ cup cooked chickpeas

Optional: Cooked rice

¼ cup minced fresh cilantro

1. Add the garlic, apple, banana, raisins, brown sugar, cumin, saffron, curry powder, broth, coconut milk, lemon or lime juice, and Worcestershire sauce to the pressure cooker; stir to combine. Lock the lid into place and bring to high pressure; maintain pressure for 10 minutes.

2. Remove from the heat and quick-release the pressure. Use an immersion blender to purée. Stir in the cream. Taste for seasoning and add more curry powder if needed.

3. Stir in the shrimp and scallops. Rinse the fish and pat dry; cut into bite-sized cubes and add to the pressure cooker along with the bell pepper and chickpeas. Lock the lid in place. Return to the heat and bring to high pressure; maintain pressure for 2 minutes. Remove from the heat and quick-release the pressure.

4. Divide the soup among 4 bowls, ladled over cooked rice if desired. Sprinkle a tablespoon of minced cilantro over each serving.

Steamed Mussels

Serves 6

2 pounds mussels, cleaned and debearded

1 tablespoon olive oil

1 white onion, peeled and chopped

1 clove garlic, peeled and smashed

½ cup dry white wine

½ cup water

1. Place mussels in the steamer basket.

2. Heat olive oil in an uncovered pressure cooker over medium-high heat. Add onion and garlic and sauté until softened (about 5 minutes). Pour the wine and water into the pressure cooker and add the steamer basket. Close and lock the lid.

3. Turn the heat up to high. When the cooker reaches pressure, lower the heat to the minimum needed to maintain pressure. Cook for 1 minute at low pressure.

4. When time is up, open the pressure cooker by quick-releasing the pressure.

5. Empty the cooked mussels from the steamer basket into the pressure cooker and mix well. Serve mussels with a generous scoop of cooking liquid.

Steamed Mussels

Red Wine–Poached Salmon

Serves 6

1 medium onion, peeled and quartered

2 cloves garlic, peeled and smashed

1 stalk celery, diced

1 bay leaf

½ teaspoon dried thyme

3½ cups water

2 cups dry red wine

2 tablespoons red wine or balsamic vinegar

½ teaspoon salt

½ teaspoon black peppercorns

1 (2½-pound) center-cut salmon roast

Optional: Lemon

1. Add all ingredients except the salmon and lemon to the pressure cooker. Lock the lid into place and bring to high pressure; maintain pressure for 10 minutes. Remove from the heat and allow pressure to release naturally for 15 minutes. Quick-release any remaining pressure.

2. Set the trivet in the pressure cooker. Put the pressure cooker over medium-high heat and bring the wine mixture to a high simmer.

3. Wrap the salmon in cheesecloth, leaving long enough ends to extend about 3". Use two sets of tongs to hold on to the 3" cheesecloth extensions and place the salmon on the trivet. Lock the lid into place and bring to high pressure; maintain pressure for 6 minutes. Remove from the heat and allow pressure to release naturally for 20 minutes.

4. Quick-release any remaining pressure. Use tongs to hold on to the 3" cheesecloth extensions to lift the salmon roast out of the pressure cooker. Set in a metal colander to allow extra moisture to drain away. When the roast is cool enough to handle, unwrap the cheesecloth. Peel away and discard any skin.

5. Transfer the salmon to a serving platter. Garnish with lemon slices or wedges if desired.

Coconut Fish Curry

Serves 6

1 tablespoon vegetable oil

6 fresh curry leaves or bay leaves

2 yellow onions, peeled and sliced

2 cloves garlic, peeled and minced

1 tablespoon freshly grated ginger

1 tablespoon ground coriander

2 teaspoons ground cumin

½ teaspoon ground turmeric

1 teaspoon cayenne pepper

½ teaspoon ground fenugreek

2 cups unsweetened coconut milk

2 green chilies, sliced into thin strips

1 medium tomato, chopped

1½ pounds fish steaks or fillets, rinsed and cut into bite-sized pieces (fresh or frozen and thawed)

2 teaspoons salt

Juice of ½ lemon

1. Heat vegetable oil in an uncovered pressure cooker over medium heat. Drop in the curry or bay leaves and lightly fry them until golden around the edges (about 1 minute). Add the onion, garlic, and ginger and sauté until the onions are soft (about 5 minutes). Add coriander, cumin, turmeric, cayenne pepper, and fenugreek and sauté them together with the onions until they have released their aroma (about 2 minutes).

2. Deglaze the pan with the coconut milk, making sure to scrape anything from the bottom and incorporate it in the sauce. Add the chilies, tomatoes, and fish. Stir delicately to coat the fish well with the mixture. Close and lock the lid.

3. Turn the heat up to high. When the cooker reaches pressure, lower the heat to the minimum needed to maintain pressure. Cook for 4–5 minutes at low pressure (or 2–3 minutes at high pressure).

4. When time is up, open the pressure cooker by quick-releasing the pressure.

5. Add salt and lemon juice just before serving.

Paprika Catfish with Fresh Tarragon

Serves 4

1 (14½-ounce) can diced tomatoes

2 teaspoons dried minced onion

¼ teaspoon onion powder

1 teaspoon dried minced garlic

¼ teaspoon garlic powder

1 teaspoon hot paprika

½ tablespoon chopped fresh tarragon

1 medium green bell pepper, seeded and diced

1 stalk celery, finely diced

1 teaspoon salt

¼ teaspoon black pepper

1 pound catfish fillets, rinsed and cut into bite-sized pieces

1. Add all ingredients except fish to the pressure cooker and stir to mix. Once mixed, add the fish on top. Close and lock the lid.

2. Turn the heat up to high. When the cooker reaches pressure, lower the heat to the minimum needed to maintain pressure. Cook for 4–5 minutes at low pressure (or 2–3 minutes at high pressure).

3. When time is up, open the pressure cooker by quick-releasing the pressure.

4. Gently stir and then taste for seasoning. Add more salt and pepper to taste if needed. Serve.

Gulf Grouper with Peppers and Tomatoes

Serves 4

1 tablespoon olive oil

1 small onion, peeled and diced

1 stalk celery, diced

1 green bell pepper, seeded and diced

1 (14½-ounce) can diced tomatoes

¼ cup water

1 tablespoon tomato paste

3–4 fresh basil leaves, torn

½ teaspoon chili powder

1½ pounds grouper fillets, rinsed and cut into bite-sized pieces

1 teaspoon salt

¼ teaspoon black pepper

1. Heat olive oil in an uncovered pressure cooker over medium heat. Add onion, celery, and green pepper and sauté for 3 minutes. Stir in undrained tomatoes, water, tomato paste, basil, and chili powder. Gently stir the fish pieces into the sauce in the pressure cooker. Close and lock the lid.

2. Turn the heat up to high. When the cooker reaches pressure, lower the heat to the minimum needed to maintain pressure. Cook for 4–5 minutes at low pressure (or 2–3 minutes at high pressure).

3. When time is up, open the pressure cooker by quick-releasing the pressure. Stir in salt and pepper and serve.

Creamed Crab

Serves 4

4 tablespoons butter

½ stalk celery, finely diced

1 small red onion, peeled and finely diced

1 pound uncooked lump crabmeat

¼ cup chicken broth

½ cup heavy cream

Salt and freshly ground black pepper, to taste

1. Melt the butter in the pressure cooker over medium heat. Add the celery; sauté for 1 minute or until celery begins to soften. Stir in the onion; sauté for 3 minutes. Stir in the crabmeat and broth.

2. Lock the lid into place and bring to low pressure; maintain for 3 minutes. Quick-release the pressure and remove the lid. Carefully stir in the cream. Taste for seasoning and add salt and pepper to taste. Serve.

Shrimp Risotto

Chapter 10: Fish and Seafood Entrées

Shrimp Risotto

Serves 4

2 tablespoons extra-virgin olive oil

1 small onion, peeled and diced

1 teaspoon fennel seeds

3 cloves garlic, peeled and minced

1½ cups Arborio rice

2 tablespoons tomato paste

Pinch saffron threads

¼ cup dry white vermouth

3 cups chicken broth

1 pound medium shrimp, peeled and deveined

Salt and freshly ground black pepper, to taste

1. Bring the oil to temperature in the pressure cooker over medium-high heat. Add the onion and fennel seeds; sauté for 3 minutes or until the onions are softened.

2. Add the garlic, rice, tomato paste, and saffron; stir until the rice is evenly colored. Stir in vermouth and broth.

3. Lock the lid into place and bring to high pressure; maintain pressure for 6 minutes. Quick-release the pressure and remove the lid.

4. Stir in the shrimp; simmer for 2 minutes or until the shrimp are pale pink and cooked through.

5. Taste for seasoning and add salt and pepper if needed. Serve immediately.

Poached Octopus

Serves 6

2 pounds potatoes (about 6 medium), washed

3 teaspoons salt, divided

Water for cooking

1 octopus (about 2 pounds), cleaned and rinsed

3 cloves garlic, peeled, divided

1 bay leaf

2 teaspoons whole peppercorns

1/2 cup olive oil

4 tablespoons white wine vinegar

1/2 teaspoon black pepper

1 bunch of parsley, chopped

1. Place the potatoes in the pressure cooker with 2 teaspoons salt and enough water to just cover the potatoes halfway. Close and lock the lid.

2. Turn the heat up to high. When the cooker reaches pressure, lower the heat to the minimum needed to maintain pressure. Cook for 10–15 minutes at high pressure.

3. When time is up, open the pressure cooker by quick-releasing the pressure.

4. Remove the potatoes with tongs (reserve the cooking water), and peel them as soon as you can handle them. Dice the potatoes into bite-sized pieces.

5. Add the octopus to the potato cooking water in the cooker, with more water to cover if needed. Add one whole garlic clove, the bay leaf, and the peppercorns. Close and lock the lid.

6. Turn the heat up to high. When the cooker reaches pressure, lower the heat to the minimum needed to maintain pressure. Cook for 15–20 minutes at high pressure.

7. While the octopus is cooking, prepare the vinaigrette. Crush the remaining garlic cloves and place in a small jar or plastic container. Add olive oil, vinegar, 1 teaspoon salt, and ground pepper. Close the lid and shake to blend.

8. When time is up, open the pressure cooker by quick-releasing the pressure.

9. Check the octopus for tenderness by seeing if a fork will sink easily into the thickest part of the flesh. If not, close the top and bring it to pressure for another minute or two and check again.

10. When the octopus is ready, remove and drain. Chop the head and tentacles into small, bite-sized chunks.

11. Right before serving, mix the potatoes with the octopus, cover with the vinaigrette, and sprinkle with parsley.

Louisiana Grouper

Serves 4

2 tablespoons peanut or vegetable oil
1 small onion, peeled and diced
1 stalk celery, diced
1 green bell pepper, seeded and diced
1 (15-ounce) can diced tomatoes
¼ cup water
1 tablespoon tomato paste
1 teaspoon sugar
Pinch dried basil
½ teaspoon chili powder
4 grouper fillets
Salt and black pepper, to taste

1. Bring the oil to temperature in the pressure cooker over medium-high heat. Add the onion, celery, and green pepper; sauté for 3 minutes. Stir in undrained tomatoes, water, tomato paste, sugar, basil, and chili powder.

2. Rinse the fish and pat dry; cut into bite-sized pieces. Sprinkle with salt and pepper, to taste. Gently stir the fish pieces into the sauce in the pressure cooker. Lock the lid into place and bring to high pressure; maintain pressure for 5 minutes. Quick-release the pressure.

Steamed Clams

Serves 6

2 pounds fresh clams, rinsed and purged

1 tablespoon olive oil

1 white onion, peeled and chopped

1 clove garlic, peeled and smashed

½ cup dry white wine

½ cup water

1. Place clams in the steamer basket.

2. Heat olive oil in an uncovered pressure cooker over medium-high heat. Add onion and garlic and sauté until softened (about 5 minutes). Pour the wine and water into the pressure cooker and add the steamer basket. Close and lock the lid.

3. Turn the heat up to high. When the cooker reaches pressure, lower the heat to the minimum needed to maintain pressure. Cook for 4–6 minutes at high pressure.

4. When time is up, open the pressure cooker by quick-releasing the pressure.

5. Empty the cooked clams from the steamer basket into the pressure cooker and mix well. Serve clams with a generous scoop of cooking liquid.

CHAPTER 11

Vegetarian Entrées

Cuban Black Beans and Rice

Serves 6

1 cup dried black beans

4 cups water

3 tablespoons olive or vegetable oil

1 medium green bell pepper, seeded and diced

$\frac{1}{2}$ stalk celery, finely diced

$\frac{1}{2}$ cup peeled and grated carrots

1 medium onion, peeled and diced

2 cloves garlic, peeled and minced

$\frac{3}{4}$ cup medium- or long-grain white rice

2 cups Vegetable Stock (see recipe in Chapter 4)

2 teaspoons paprika

$\frac{1}{2}$ teaspoon cumin

$\frac{1}{4}$ teaspoon chili powder

1 bay leaf

Salt and freshly ground black pepper, to taste

1. Rinse the beans and add them to a covered container. Pour in the water, cover, and let the beans soak overnight. Drain.

2. Bring the oil to temperature in the pressure cooker over medium-high heat. Add the green bell pepper, celery, and carrots; sauté for 2 minutes. Add the onion; sauté for 3 minutes or until the onions are soft. Stir in the garlic and sauté for 30 seconds.

3. Stir in the rice and stir-fry until the rice begins to brown. Add the drained beans, stock, paprika, cumin, chili powder, and bay leaf.

4. Lock the lid into place and bring to low pressure; maintain pressure for 18 minutes. Remove from the heat and allow pressure to release naturally. Stir, taste for seasoning, and add salt and pepper to taste. Remove bay leaf and serve.

Risotto Primavera

Serves 4

1 tablespoon extra-virgin olive oil

1 tablespoon unsalted butter

2 medium carrots, peeled and finely diced

1 stalk celery, finely diced

2 large shallots or 1 small red onion, peeled and diced

1 clove garlic, peeled and minced

½ teaspoon dried basil

1 teaspoon dried parsley

2 cups Arborio rice

½ cup dry white wine or vermouth

5 cups vegetable or mushroom broth, divided

½ pound asparagus

1 cup peas

1 cup shredded snow peas

1 cup peeled, seeded, and diced zucchini

1 cup shredded fontina cheese

½ cup grated Parmigiano-Reggiano or Asiago cheese

1. Bring the oil and butter to temperature in the pressure cooker over medium heat. Add the carrot and celery; sauté for 3 minutes. Add the shallots or red onion; sauté for 3 minutes or until the vegetables are tender. Add the garlic, basil, and parsley; sauté for 30 seconds.

2. Stir in the rice and stir-fry for 4 minutes or until the rice becomes opaque. Add the wine or vermouth; cook and stir for 3 minutes or until the liquid is absorbed by the rice. Stir in 4½ cups broth.

3. Lock the lid into place and bring to high pressure; maintain pressure for 6 minutes. Quick-release the pressure and remove the lid.

4. Stir in the remaining ½ cup broth. Once the broth is absorbed and the rice is fluffed, adjust heat to maintain a simmer.

5. Clean the asparagus and cut it into 1" pieces. Add the asparagus, peas, snow peas, and zucchini. Stir and cook until the vegetables are bright green and cooked through. Stir in the cheese. Serve.

Sweet and Sour "Meatballs"

Yield: 12 "meatballs"

½ cup white sugar

2 tablespoons pineapple juice

⅓ cup white vinegar

⅔ cup water

2 tablespoons soy sauce

2 tablespoons vegetarian
Worcestershire sauce

1 tablespoon ketchup

2 tablespoons cornstarch

1 pound vegetarian ground beef, such
as Gimme Lean Beef

½ onion, peeled and diced

1 clove garlic, peeled and minced

½ cup panko bread crumbs

1. In the pressure cooker, bring the sugar, pineapple juice, vinegar, water, soy sauce, Worcestershire sauce, ketchup, and cornstarch to a boil over high heat. Stir continuously until the mixture has thickened, then remove from heat.

2. In a large mixing bowl, combine the vegetarian ground beef, onion, garlic, and bread crumbs, and mix until well combined. (Using your hands is the easiest method.)

3. Roll the "beef" mixture into 12 meatballs; add them to the sauce in the pressure cooker.

4. Lock the lid into place. Bring to high pressure; maintain pressure for 5 minutes. Quick-release the pressure, then remove the lid. Serve warm.

Ratatouille

Serves 4

2 tablespoons extra-virgin olive oil

2 (7") zucchini, washed and sliced

1 Japanese eggplant, peeled and sliced

1 small onion, peeled and thinly sliced

1 green bell pepper, seeded and diced

2 medium potatoes, peeled and diced

8 ounces fresh mushrooms, cleaned and sliced

1 (28-ounce) can diced tomatoes

3 tablespoons tomato paste

3 tablespoons water

2 cloves garlic, peeled and minced

2 teaspoons Mrs. Dash Italian Medley Seasoning Blend

1/8 teaspoon dried red pepper flakes

Salt and freshly ground black pepper, to taste

Parmigiano-Reggiano cheese, grated

1. Coat the bottom and sides of the pressure cooker with oil. Add the remaining ingredients except cheese in layers in the order given. Lock the lid into place and bring to low pressure; maintain pressure for 6 minutes.

2. Remove from heat and quick-release the pressure. Remove the lid, stir, and taste for seasoning, adjusting if necessary. Serve topped with the grated cheese.

Herb and Quinoa Stuffed Tomatoes

Serves 4

1 cup water

4 large tomatoes

1 cup cooked quinoa

1 stalk celery, chopped

1 tablespoon minced garlic

2 tablespoons chopped, fresh oregano

2 tablespoons chopped, fresh parsley

½ teaspoon salt

¼ teaspoon black pepper

1. Place water in the pressure cooker and add the steamer basket.

2. Remove the core from each tomato and discard. Scoop out the seeds, leaving the walls of the tomato intact.

3. In a small bowl, stir together the quinoa, celery, garlic, oregano, parsley, salt, and pepper. Divide evenly among the four tomatoes. Place the filled tomatoes in a single layer in the steamer basket. Close and lock the lid.

4. Turn the heat up to high. When the cooker reaches pressure, lower the heat to the minimum needed to maintain pressure. Cook for 5–7 minutes at high pressure.

5. When time is up, open the pressure cooker by quick-releasing the pressure. Gently lift out the steamer basket and, using tongs or two spoons, place each tomato (they will be very delicate) on individual plates.

Herb and Quinoa Stuffed Tomatoes

Ricotta-Stuffed Zucchini

Serves 6

3 large, thick zucchini

2 tablespoons olive oil, divided

2 garlic cloves, peeled and pressed

1/2 teaspoon salt

1/4 teaspoon black pepper

1 cup fresh ricotta cheese

1/2 cup unseasoned bread crumbs

1 bunch thyme, woody stems removed and leaves chopped

1 bunch oregano, woody stems removed and leaves chopped

1 medium onion, peeled and chopped

1 (14 1/2-ounce) can chopped tomatoes

1 bunch basil, chopped

1/2 cup water

1. Slice the zucchini in $1^1/_2$"-thick rounds. Scoop out the insides of each round to $^3/_4$ the depth (about 1" deep) to make little cups. Reserve zucchini flesh and set aside.

2. Heat 1 tablespoon olive oil in an uncovered pressure cooker over medium heat. Add the reserved zucchini flesh, garlic, salt, and pepper. Cook until zucchini is softened (about 8 minutes), remove from pressure cooker, and set aside in a mixing bowl. Add ricotta, bread crumbs, thyme, and oregano to bowl and mix well.

3. Stuff the zucchini cups with the zucchini-ricotta mixture.

4. Return the pressure cooker to medium heat. Add another tablespoon of olive oil and sauté the onions until softened (about 5 minutes). Add the tomatoes, basil, and water.

5. Lower the steamer basket into the pressure cooker over the sauce. Carefully place the stuffed zucchini cups in the basket. Close and lock the lid.

6. Turn the heat up to high. When the cooker reaches pressure, lower the heat to the minimum needed to maintain pressure. Cook for 5 minutes at high pressure.

7. When time is up, open the pressure cooker by quick-releasing the pressure.

8. Using tongs, carefully remove the zucchini cups to a serving platter. Pour tomato sauce over zucchini cups and serve.

Roasted Vegetable Burger

Serves 2–4

1 cup dried black beans

8 cups water

2 tablespoons vegetable oil, divided

1 teaspoon salt, plus more to taste

½ medium yellow onion, peeled and chopped

½ red bell pepper, seeded and chopped

½ cup chopped yellow squash

½ zucchini, chopped

4 cloves garlic, peeled and minced

1 tablespoon extra-virgin olive oil

½ jalapeño, seeded and minced

½ cup panko bread crumbs

Black pepper, to taste

1. Add the beans and 4 cups water to the pressure cooker. Lock the lid into place; bring to high pressure for 1 minute. Remove from the heat and quick-release the pressure.

2. Drain the water, rinse the beans, and add to the pressure cooker again with the remaining 4 cups of water. Let soak for 1 hour.

3. Add 1 tablespoon vegetable oil and 1 teaspoon salt. Lock the lid into place; bring to high pressure and maintain for 12 minutes. Remove from the heat and allow pressure to release naturally. Drain the beans and set aside.

4. Preheat the oven to 450°F. Toss the onion, bell pepper, yellow squash, zucchini, and garlic in the olive oil. Place on a baking sheet and cook for 30–35 minutes in the oven, turning once.

5. Pour the beans into a large bowl and add the rest of the ingredients except remaining 1 tablespoon vegetable oil. Mash the mixture with a potato masher. Form the bean mixture into burger patties. Add the remaining oil to a pan and cook the burgers until they are browned on both sides.

Gnocchi and Mushrooms in
Rosemary Alfredo Sauce

Chapter 11: Vegetarian Entrées

Gnocchi and Mushrooms in Rosemary Alfredo Sauce

Serves 2–3

Water, as needed

16 ounces uncooked gnocchi

1 tablespoon extra-virgin olive oil

1/2 cup sliced mushrooms

1 teaspoon fresh lemon juice

2 cups béchamel sauce, or vegan version of béchamel sauce

1/2 cup Parmesan cheese, or vegan shredded Parmesan or mozzarella

1/2 cup diced tomatoes

1 teaspoon chopped fresh rosemary

Salt and black pepper, to taste

1. Fill the pressure cooker with enough water to cover the gnocchi. Bring the water to a boil. Add the gnocchi. Lock the lid into place and bring to high pressure; maintain pressure for 1 minute. Use the natural release method to release the pressure and then remove the lid. Drain the gnocchi and set aside.

2. Add the olive oil to a pan over medium heat and sauté the mushrooms for about 1 minute. Add the gnocchi and sauté for 1 minute more.

3. Deglaze the pan with the lemon juice, then add the béchamel sauce and Parmesan cheese, and allow it to reduce until desired consistency is reached.

4. Stir in the tomatoes and rosemary. Taste for seasoning, and add salt and pepper, if necessary.

BBQ Tempeh Burger

Serves 4–6

1 cup lentils

1 (8-ounce) package tempeh, crumbled

4$\frac{1}{2}$ cups water

1 tablespoon vegetable oil

1 teaspoon salt, plus more to taste

$\frac{1}{2}$ cup flour

$\frac{1}{2}$ cup mustard

$\frac{1}{4}$ cup sugar

$\frac{1}{8}$ cup brown sugar

$\frac{1}{4}$ cup cider vinegar

1 tablespoon chili powder

$\frac{1}{8}$ teaspoon cayenne pepper

$\frac{1}{2}$ teaspoon soy sauce

1 tablespoon butter, melted, or vegan margarine, such as Earth Balance

$\frac{1}{2}$ tablespoon liquid smoke

Black pepper, to taste

1. Add the lentils, tempeh, water, oil, and 1 teaspoon salt to the pressure cooker.

2. Lock the lid into place; bring to high pressure and maintain for 7 minutes. Remove from the heat and allow pressure to release naturally. Drain the lentils and tempeh and add to a large mixing bowl.

3. Combine the rest of the ingredients with the lentils and tempeh. Mash the mixture with a potato masher. Form the tempeh mixture into burger patties.

4. Preheat the oven to 350°F. Place the burgers on a greased baking sheet. Bake in the oven for 25–30 minutes, flipping after 15 minutes.

"Bacon" and Avocado Burger

Serves 4

1 cup dried black beans

8 cups water

2 tablespoons vegetable oil, divided

1 teaspoon salt

1 jalapeño, seeded and minced

3 cloves garlic, peeled and minced

½ medium yellow onion, peeled and diced

1 tablespoon chili powder

1 tablespoon cumin

½ cup panko bread crumbs

¼ cup chopped fresh parsley

Salt and black pepper, to taste

8–12 pieces of tempeh bacon

1 avocado, sliced

1. Add the beans and 4 cups water to the pressure cooker. Lock the lid into place; bring to high pressure for 1 minute. Remove from the heat and quick-release the pressure.

2. Drain the water, rinse the beans, and add to the pressure cooker again with the remaining 4 cups of water. Let soak for 1 hour.

3. Add 1 tablespoon of the vegetable oil and salt. Lock the lid into place; bring to high pressure and maintain for 12 minutes. Remove from the heat and allow pressure to release naturally. Drain the beans.

4. Pour the beans into a large bowl and add the rest of the ingredients except remaining oil, tempeh bacon, and avocado. Mash the mixture with a potato masher. Form the bean mixture into burger patties. Add the remaining oil to a pan and cook the burgers until they are browned on both sides.

5. Top each of the burgers with tempeh bacon and avocado slices.

Smoked Portobello Burger

Serves 4

4 large portobello mushroom caps

¼ cup red wine vinegar

2 tablespoons extra-virgin olive oil

1 tablespoon minced shallots

½ tablespoon soy sauce

Salt and black pepper, to taste

1 cup water

1 tablespoon liquid smoke

1. Place the mushrooms in a shallow dish. In a small bowl, mix the red wine vinegar, olive oil, shallots, soy sauce, salt, and pepper. Pour the mixture over the mushrooms and allow them to marinate for about 20 minutes, turning 2–3 times throughout.

2. Pour the water and liquid smoke into the pressure cooker and place the steamer tray inside. Place the mushrooms on top of the steamer tray.

3. Lock the lid into place; bring to high pressure and maintain for 5 minutes. Remove from the heat and allow pressure to release naturally.

Smoked Portobello Burger

Chapter 11: Vegetarian Entrées

Quinoa Burger

Serves 2

½ cup quinoa

1 cup water

1 carrot, peeled and shredded

½ medium yellow onion, peeled and diced

2 (15-ounce) cans white beans, drained

1 egg, beaten, or 2 teaspoons cornstarch combined with 2 tablespoons warm water

1 tablespoon cumin

1 teaspoon dried sage or basil

Salt and black pepper, to taste

1 tablespoon olive oil

1. Add the quinoa and water to the pressure cooker.

2. Lock the lid into place; bring to high pressure and maintain for 6 minutes. Remove from the heat and allow pressure to release naturally. Fluff with a fork.

3. In a large bowl, combine all the ingredients except olive oil and mash with a potato masher. Form the mixture into patties.

4. Add the olive oil to a pan and cook the burgers until they are browned on each side.

Orzo-Stuffed Poblano Peppers

Serves 4

Water, as needed

½ cup orzo pasta

¼ cup diced medium yellow onions

¼ cup diced tomatoes

1 clove garlic, peeled and minced

2 tablespoons chopped fresh cilantro

1 tablespoon extra-virgin olive oil

Salt and black pepper, to taste

4 large poblano peppers

1. Preheat the oven to 350°F. Fill the pressure cooker with enough water to cover the pasta. Bring the water to a boil. Add the pasta. Lock the lid into place and bring to high pressure; maintain pressure for 3 minutes. Use the natural release method to release the pressure and then remove the lid. Drain the pasta.

2. In a medium bowl, combine the orzo, onions, tomatoes, garlic, cilantro, olive oil, salt, and pepper. Stir until combined.

3. Place the poblano peppers on a flat surface and cut out a long triangular portion from the top (stem to tip) to make room for the filling. Remove the seeds.

4. Fill each pepper with the orzo mixture and put the triangular piece of pepper back in place, covering the hole. Place on a baking sheet.

5. Bake for 45–50 minutes, or until tender.

Pasta Puttanesca

Serves 6–8

Water, as needed

1 pound linguine

2 teaspoons olive oil

2 garlic cloves, peeled and slivered

1 tablespoon chopped fresh basil

2 tablespoons capers

¼ cup kalamata olives, pitted and halved

1 teaspoon dried red pepper flakes

1 tablespoon brine (juice from the olives)

1 (14-ounce) can crushed tomatoes, drained

Salt and black pepper, to taste

1. Fill the pressure cooker with enough water to cover the pasta. Bring the water to a boil. Add the pasta. Lock the lid into place and bring to high pressure; maintain pressure for 6 minutes. Use the natural release method to release the pressure and then remove the lid. Drain with a colander and set the pasta aside.

2. In a sauté pan over medium heat, warm the oil. Add the garlic and cook for 2–3 minutes. Stir in the basil, capers, olives, and red pepper flakes and cook for 2 more minutes.

3. Stir in the brine and crushed tomatoes and simmer over low heat for 10–15 minutes. Season with salt and pepper to taste.

4. Combine the sauce with the linguine and serve.

Whole-Wheat Fettuccine with Mushroom Cream Sauce

Serves 6–8

Water, as needed

1 pound whole-wheat fettuccine

2 tablespoons butter, or vegan margarine, such as Earth Balance, divided

1 cup sliced mushrooms (try button, shiitake, oyster, or portobello)

2 cloves garlic, peeled and minced

1 tablespoon all-purpose flour

1¼ cups milk, or unsweetened soymilk

1 tablespoon chopped fresh parsley

1 tablespoon fresh lemon juice

Salt and black pepper, to taste

1. Fill the pressure cooker with enough water to cover the pasta. Bring the water to a boil. Add the pasta. Lock the lid into place and bring to high pressure; maintain pressure for 7 minutes. Use the natural release method to release the pressure and then remove the lid. Set the pasta aside.

2. Melt 1 tablespoon of the butter in a sauté pan, then add the mushrooms and garlic. Sauté until the mushrooms are soft, about 4 minutes. Remove from the pan and set aside.

3. Melt the second tablespoon of butter, then stir in the flour and cook for about 1 minute to make a roux. Gradually stir in the milk, stirring continuously until smooth.

4. Add the cooked mushrooms, parsley, lemon juice, salt, and pepper and cook for 1–2 minutes.

5. Pour the sauce over warm pasta and serve immediately.

Broccoli–Pine Nut Pasta Salad

Serves 6–8

Water, as needed

1 pound rotini pasta

1/3 cup pine nuts, toasted

1 head broccoli, blanched and chopped

1 red bell pepper, seeded and chopped

1/2 medium yellow onion, peeled and diced

2 cloves garlic, peeled and minced

2 tablespoons red wine vinegar

1/3 cup extra-virgin olive oil

Salt and black pepper, to taste

1. Fill the pressure cooker with enough water to cover the pasta. Bring the water to a boil. Add the pasta. Lock the lid into place and bring to high pressure; maintain pressure for 7 minutes. Use the natural release method to release the pressure and then remove the lid. Drain the pasta and run cold water over it until cooled. Set the pasta aside.

2. In a sauté pan over low heat, toast the pine nuts until they are golden brown. Be careful not to burn them.

3. In a large bowl, combine the pine nuts, broccoli, red pepper, onion, garlic, vinegar, olive oil, and pasta. Taste for seasoning and add salt and pepper if needed.

Pasta Salad with Tomato, Arugula, and Feta

Serves 6–8

Water, as needed

1 pound rotini pasta

2 Roma tomatoes, diced

2 garlic cloves, peeled and minced

1 red bell pepper, seeded and diced

2 tablespoons white wine vinegar

1/3 cup extra-virgin olive oil

2 cups chopped arugula or spinach

1 cup feta cheese or vegan feta cheese

Salt and black pepper, to taste

1. Fill the pressure cooker with enough water to cover the pasta. Bring the water to a boil. Add the pasta. Lock the lid into place and bring to high pressure; maintain pressure for 7 minutes. Use the natural release method to release the pressure and then remove the lid. Drain the pasta, then run cold water over the pasta until cooled. Set aside.

2. In a large bowl, mix the tomatoes, garlic, red bell pepper, vinegar, olive oil, arugula or spinach, and feta. Mix in the pasta and add salt and pepper to taste.

Fresh Spinach–White Wine Angel Hair Pasta

Serves 6–8

Water, as needed

1 pound angel hair pasta

1 tablespoon olive oil

¼ yellow onion, peeled and diced

2 cloves garlic, peeled and minced

½ cup white wine

¼ cup water, or as needed

1 tablespoon butter, or vegan margarine, such as Earth Balance

1 tablespoon flour

Salt and black pepper, to taste

1 cup steamed spinach

1. Fill the pressure cooker with enough water to cover the pasta. Bring the water to a boil. Add the pasta. Lock the lid into place and bring to high pressure; maintain pressure for 4 minutes. Use the natural release method to release the pressure and then remove the lid. Drain and set the pasta aside.

2. In a medium saucepan over low heat, add the olive oil, onion, and garlic. Cook until the onions are soft, about 5 minutes. Add the white wine and water, then bring to a low simmer. Continue simmering for about 10 minutes.

3. Add the butter and flour, stirring until completely combined and the sauce begins to thicken. If the sauce becomes too thick, add more water until you reach the desired consistency, then season with salt and pepper.

4. In a large mixing bowl, combine the spinach, pasta, and white-wine sauce, then toss until the pasta is completely coated.

Bowtie Pasta in a Sage Beurre Blanc Sauce

Serves 6–8

Water, as needed

1 pound bowtie pasta

1 tablespoon extra-virgin olive oil

1 cup sliced white mushrooms

1 small red onion, peeled and julienned

2 cloves garlic, peeled and minced

1 cup white wine

2 tablespoons white wine vinegar

¾ cup cold butter, or vegan margarine, such as Earth Balance

1 cup diced tomatoes

1 teaspoon dried sage

Salt and black pepper, to taste

1. Fill the pressure cooker with enough water to cover the pasta. Bring the water to a boil. Add the pasta. Lock the lid into place and bring to high pressure; maintain pressure for 5 minutes. Use the natural release method to release the pressure and then remove the lid. Drain and set the pasta aside.

2. Add the olive oil to a pan over medium heat and sauté the mushrooms and onion until golden brown. Add the garlic and sauté for an additional 30 seconds. Add the wine and vinegar, and let reduce for about 3 minutes. Add the cold butter to the pan, 1 tablespoon at a time, stirring the butter constantly into the wine to create an emulsion.

3. Once the butter has emulsified, add the tomatoes, sage, and salt and pepper, to taste. Toss with the pasta before serving.

CHAPTER 12

Sweets and Desserts

Chocolate-Berry Bread Pudding

Serves 6

6 slices day-old challah or brioche

½ cup raspberry preserves

½ cup diced dried strawberries or prunes

½ cup chopped hazelnuts

½ cup cocoa

½ cup sugar

Pinch salt

2 tablespoons butter, melted

3 large eggs

2 cups whole milk

2 cups heavy cream

1 tablespoon vanilla extract

1 cup water

1. If the crusts on the bread are dark, remove them; their overpowering flavor will be a distraction. If using fresh bread, lightly toast it to dry it out. Spread the raspberry preserves over the bread.

2. Treat a 5-cup or larger heatproof soufflé dish that will fit inside the pressure cooker with nonstick spray.

3. Tear the bread into chunks and add half of it preserves side up over the bottom of the soufflé dish. Sprinkle the dried fruit and chopped hazelnuts over the bread. Add the remaining bread preserves side down over the top.

4. Add the cocoa, sugar, and salt to a large measuring cup. Whisk thoroughly. Add the butter and eggs; whisk to mix. Whisk in the milk, cream, and vanilla.

5. Pour half of the cocoa mixture over the bread. Tap down the dish to remove any air bubbles and wait several minutes for the bread to absorb the liquid. Pour in the remaining cocoa mixture.

6. Tear off 2 large pieces of heavy-duty aluminum foil, each large enough to wrap around the soufflé dish. Lay one piece of the foil over the top of the dish, crimping it slightly around the edges, and wrap it around the dish, folding it and tucking it under. Set the dish in the middle of the remaining piece of foil; bring it up and over the top of the dish and crimp to seal.

Chocolate-Berry Bread Pudding—continued

7. Pour the water into the pressure cooker. Set the rack in the pressure cooker. Crisscross 2 long doubled pieces of foil over the rack to help you lift the dish out of the pressure cooker later. Place the covered soufflé dish over the crossed foil strips on the rack.

8. Lock the lid into place and bring to high pressure; maintain pressure for 15 minutes. Remove from the heat and allow pressure to release naturally.

9. Remove the dish from the pressure cooker, remove the foil, and place on a rack until ready to serve or until it's cool enough to cover and refrigerate. Serve warm or chilled.

Piña Colada Bread Pudding

Serves 8

1 (16-ounce) can cream of coconut

1 cup heavy cream, or soymilk

3 large eggs, or 3 ounces silken tofu

$1/2$ cup butter, melted, or vegan margarine, such as Earth Balance

$3/4$ cup sugar

$1 1/2$ teaspoons rum flavoring

$1/4$ teaspoon ground nutmeg

1 (20-ounce) can pineapple chunks, drained

$1 1/4$ cups coconut

8 cups French bread, torn into 2" cubes

$1 1/2$ cups water

1. Add the cream of coconut, cream, eggs, butter, sugar, rum flavoring, and nutmeg to a large bowl. Whisk to mix thoroughly. Stir in the drained pineapple and coconut. Fold in the bread cubes.

2. Treat a 5-cup soufflé dish with nonstick spray. Transfer the bread pudding mixture into the dish. Pour in the water and place the rack into the pressure cooker.

3. Crisscross long, doubled strips of foil over the rack to create handles to use later to remove the pan.

4. Treat one side of a 15"-square piece of heavy-duty aluminum foil with nonstick spray. Lay the foil, treated side down, over the soufflé dish and crimp the edges to seal.

5. Tear off another piece of heavy-duty foil to completely wrap the soufflé dish to ensure the seal. Place over the crisscrossed pieces of foil.

6. Lock the lid into place and bring to high pressure; maintain pressure for 12 minutes. Remove pressure cooker from heat, quick-release pressure, and remove lid.

7. Remove pan from the pressure cooker, uncover, and place on a wire rack to cool. Serve warm, at room temperature, or chilled.

Cinnamon Brown Rice Pudding with Raisins

Serves 2

1 cup short-grain brown rice
1⅓ cups water
1 tablespoon vanilla extract
1 cinnamon stick
1 tablespoon butter
1 cup raisins
3 tablespoons honey
½ cup heavy cream

1. Add rice, water, vanilla, cinnamon stick, and butter to the pressure cooker. Close and lock the lid.

2. Turn the heat up to high. When the cooker reaches pressure, lower the heat to the minimum needed to maintain pressure. Cook for 20–22 minutes at high pressure.

3. Open with the natural release method—move the pressure cooker to a cool burner and wait for the pressure to come down on its own (about 10 minutes). For electric pressure cookers, disengage the "keep warm" mode or unplug the cooker. After 10 minutes, release the rest of the pressure using the valve.

4. Remove the cinnamon stick and stir in the raisins, honey, and cream.

5. Let stand 5 minutes, then serve warm.

Coconut Custard

Serves 8

1 cup milk

1 (14-ounce) can coconut milk

1 (10-ounce) can sweetened condensed milk

½ teaspoon vanilla extract

3 eggs

3 egg yolks

2 cups water

1. Add the milk, coconut milk, and sweetened condensed milk to a saucepan. Heat it over medium heat until it's steaming and begins to reach a low boil.

2. Stir in the vanilla. In a separate bowl whisk the eggs together with the egg yolks.

3. Whisk a couple of tablespoons of the milk mixture into the eggs and then stir the eggs into the milk mixture.

4. Reduce heat to low; cook and stir for 4 minutes or until the mixture begins to thicken.

5. Treat a 6-cup soufflé dish with nonstick spray. Pour the heated custard into the treated dish.

6. Cover the dish with a piece of heavy-duty aluminum foil; crimp the edges to form a seal around the dish.

7. Pour the water and place the rack into the pressure cooker. Crisscross long, doubled strips of foil over the rack to create handles to use later to remove the pan.

8. Place the pan on the rack over the foil strips. Lock the lid into place and bring to high pressure; maintain pressure for 30 minutes.

9. Remove from heat and allow pressure to release naturally for 30 minutes. Quick-release any remaining pressure. Remove the lid.

Coconut Custard—continued

10. Lift the pan from the pressure cooker and place it on a cooling rack. Once the custard has cooled, remove the foil.

11. Use a paper towel to dab any moisture that may have formed on the surface of the custard. Cover the dish with plastic wrap and refrigerate until ready to serve.

Amaretti-Stuffed Apricots

Serves 6

3 apricots, mature but lightly firm

1 cup crumbled amaretti cookies (about 8 cookies)

2 tablespoons almonds

1 teaspoon lemon zest

2 tablespoons butter, melted

1 cup red wine

4 tablespoons sugar

1. Wash the apricots well, slice them in half, and remove the pit. Make the hole a little deeper with the large end of a melon baller.

2. Crumble the cookies and almonds in a chopper, then stir in the lemon zest and butter.

3. Place wine and sugar in the pressure cooker and add the steamer basket. Fill the apricots with the cookie crumble filling and place carefully in the steamer basket. Close and lock the lid.

4. Turn the heat up to high. When the cooker reaches pressure, lower the heat to the minimum needed to maintain pressure. Cook for 3 minutes at high pressure.

5. When time is up, open the pressure cooker by quick-releasing the pressure.

6. Carefully remove the apricots with tongs. If you like, you can reduce the red wine in the pan (uncovered) and use it as a syrupy sauce.

7. Serve at room temperature or chilled.

Fresh Figs Poached in Wine

Serves 6

1 cup sweet red wine

1 pound fresh figs

1/2 cup sugar or honey

1/2 cup pine nuts

1. Add wine to the base of the pressure cooker. Stand the figs in the cooker. Close and lock the lid.

2. Turn the heat up to high. When the cooker reaches pressure, lower the heat to the minimum needed to maintain pressure. Cook for 3 minutes at low pressure (1 minute at high pressure).

3. When time is up, open the pressure cooker by quick-releasing the pressure.

4. Carefully move figs to serving platter or individual dessert dishes.

5. Add sugar to the cooking liquid and cook on high heat, uncovered, to reduce the contents of the cooker to about half. Drizzle figs with a spoonful of the syrup, or more if you like, and sprinkle with pine nuts.

6. Serve warm or chilled.

Maple Dessert Bread

Serves 8

½ cup unbleached all-purpose flour
½ cup stone-ground cornmeal
½ cup whole-wheat flour
½ teaspoon baking powder
¼ teaspoon fine salt
¼ teaspoon baking soda
½ cup maple syrup
½ cup buttermilk
1 large egg
2 cups water

1. Add the all-purpose flour, cornmeal, whole-wheat flour, baking powder, salt, and baking soda to a mixing bowl. Stir to combine.

2. Add the maple syrup, buttermilk, and egg to another mixing bowl. Whisk to mix, then pour into the flour mixture. Mix until a thick batter is formed.

3. Butter the inside of a 6-cup heatproof pudding mold or baking pan. Pour the batter into the dish and cover tightly with foil.

4. Prepare the pressure cooker by filling it with water and inserting the trivet or steamer basket. Make a foil sling by folding a long piece of foil into three and lower the covered dish into the pressure cooker. Close and lock the lid.

5. Turn the heat up to high. When the cooker reaches pressure, lower the heat to the minimum needed to maintain pressure. Cook for 40–45 minutes at high pressure.

6. Open with the natural release method—move the pressure cooker to a cool burner and wait for the pressure to come down on its own (about 10 minutes). For electric pressure cookers, disengage the "keep warm" mode or unplug the cooker. After 10 minutes, release the rest of the pressure using the valve.

7. Remove lid. Lift pan from pressure cooker and place on a cooling rack. Remove foil.

Maple Dessert Bread—continued

8. Check if the bread is done by inserting a toothpick into its center. It's done if the toothpick comes out clean. If the toothpick comes out wet, place the foil over the pan and return it to the pressure cooker for 5 more minutes at high pressure, repeating if necessary.

9. Use a knife to loosen the bread and invert it onto the cooling rack. Serve the bread warm.

Lemon Cheesecake

Chapter 12: Sweets and Desserts

Lemon Cheesecake

Serves 8

Nonstick spray

12 gingersnaps or vanilla wafers

1½ tablespoons almonds, toasted

½ tablespoon butter, melted

2 (8-ounce) packages cream cheese, room temperature

½ cup sugar

2 large eggs

Zest of 1 lemon, grated

1 tablespoon fresh lemon juice

½ teaspoon natural lemon extract

1 teaspoon vanilla extract

2 cups water

1. Use a pressure cooker with a rack that's large enough to hold a 7" × 3" springform pan. Treat the inside of the pan with nonstick spray.

2. Add the cookies and almonds to a food processor. Pulse to create cookie crumbs and chop the nuts. Add the melted butter and pulse to mix.

3. Transfer the crumb mixture to the springform pan and press down into the pan. Wipe out the food processor bowl.

4. Cut the cream cheese into cubes and add it to the food processor along with the sugar; process until smooth.

5. Add the eggs, lemon zest, lemon juice, lemon extract, and vanilla. Process for 10 seconds.

6. Scrape down the bowl and then process for another 10 seconds or until the batter is well mixed and smooth.

7. Place the springform pan in the center of two 16" × 16" pieces of aluminum foil. Crimp the foil to seal the bottom of the pan.

8. Transfer the cheesecake batter into the springform pan. Treat one side of a 10" square of aluminum foil with nonstick spray; lay over the top of the springform pan and crimp around the edges.

9. Bring the bottom foil up the sides so that it can be grasped to raise and lower the pan into and out of the pressure cooker.

10. Pour the water into the pressure cooker. Insert the rack. Set the springform pan holding the cheesecake batter on the rack.

11. Lock the lid into place and bring to high pressure; maintain pressure for 8 minutes. Remove from heat and allow pressure to release naturally. Remove the lid.

12. Lift the covered springform pan out of the pressure cooker and place on a wire rack. Remove the top foil.

13. If any moisture has accumulated on top of the cheesecake, dab it with a piece of paper towel to remove it. Let cool to room temperature and then remove from the springform pan.

Brown Betty Apple Dessert

Serves 6

2 cups dry bread crumbs

½ cup sugar

1 teaspoon cinnamon

Juice and zest of 1 lemon

1 cup olive oil, divided

8 apples, peeled, cored, and diced

2 cups water

1. Combine crumbs, sugar, cinnamon, lemon juice, lemon zest, and ½ cup oil in a mixing bowl. Set aside.

2. In a greased ovensafe dish that will fit in your cooker loosely, add a thin layer of crumbs, then one of diced apples. Continue filling the container with alternating layers of crumbs and apples until all ingredients are finished. Pour ½ cup olive oil on top.

3. Prepare the pressure cooker by filling it with 2 cups of water and inserting the trivet or steamer basket. Make a foil sling by folding a long piece of foil into three and lower the uncovered container into the pressure cooker. Close and lock the lid.

4. Turn the heat up to high. When the cooker reaches pressure, lower the heat to the minimum needed to maintain pressure. Cook for 15–20 minutes at high pressure.

5. Open with the natural release method—move the pressure cooker to a cool burner and wait for the pressure to come down on its own (about 10 minutes). For electric pressure cookers, disengage the "keep warm" mode or unplug the cooker. After 10 minutes, release the rest of the pressure using the valve.

6. Pull dish out carefully and let stand for 5 minutes before serving.

Crème Brûlée

Chapter 12: Sweets and Desserts

Crème Brûlée

Serves 6

1 cup whole milk

1 cup heavy cream

1 vanilla bean, sliced in half

2 cups water

1 teaspoon vegetable oil

6 egg yolks

⅔ cup granulated sugar

2 tablespoons demerara or raw sugar

1. In a heavy-bottomed saucepan, heat milk, cream, and vanilla bean over medium heat. Stir occasionally until the mixture begins to bubble. Turn off the heat and let cool (about 20–30 minutes). Remove the vanilla bean and scrape the seeds into the mixture.

2. In the meantime, prepare the pressure cooker by filling it with water and inserting the trivet or steamer basket. Oil 6 teacups or ramekins.

3. In a mixing bowl, whisk the egg yolks and granulated sugar until the sugar is dissolved. Slowly pour in the cooled milk mixture and incorporate it into the yolks. Whisk lightly, but do not whip the mixture.

4. Pour mixture into cups, cover with foil, and arrange in steamer basket so that all are sitting straight. You can stack some of the cups on top in a second layer. Close and lock the lid.

5. Turn the heat up to high. When the cooker reaches pressure, lower the heat to the minimum needed to maintain pressure. Cook for 5–8 minutes at high pressure.

6. Open with the natural release method—move the pressure cooker to a cool burner and wait for the pressure to come down on its own (about 10 minutes). For electric pressure cookers, disengage the "keep warm" mode or unplug the cooker. After 10 minutes, release the rest of the pressure using the valve.

7. Carefully lift out the custards. Open the first and jiggle it a bit. It should be nearly solid (they will solidify further when chilled). Remove the custards and leave to cool uncovered for about 30–45 minutes. Then, cover with plastic wrap and refrigerate for 3–24 hours.

8. Immediately before serving, sprinkle the top of the custards with demerara sugar. Caramelize the sugar by sliding custards under the broiler or by scorching the top with a culinary torch.

Cornmeal Cake

Serves 6

2 cups milk

¼ cup light brown sugar, packed

1 teaspoon orange zest, grated

½ cup fine yellow cornmeal

1 large egg

2 egg yolks

2 tablespoons butter, melted

2 tablespoons orange marmalade

1 cup water

1. Heat the milk in a saucepan over medium heat until it reaches a simmer. Stir in the brown sugar; simmer and stir until the milk is at a low boil.

2. Whisk in the orange zest and cornmeal. Simmer and stir for 2 minutes or until thickened. Remove from heat.

3. In a small bowl or measuring cup, whisk together the egg, egg yolks, butter, and orange marmalade. Stir the egg mixture into the cornmeal mixture.

4. Treat a 1-quart soufflé or heatproof glass dish with non-stick spray. Transfer the cornmeal batter to the prepared dish.

5. Pour the water into the pressure cooker and add the rack. Place the soufflé dish on the rack.

6. Lock the lid into place and bring to low pressure; maintain pressure for 12 minutes. Remove from the heat and allow pressure to release naturally for 10 minutes.

7. Quick-release any remaining pressure and remove the lid. Transfer the dish to a wire rack.

Crème Caramel

Serves 6

2²/₃ cups granulated sugar, divided

2 cups whole milk

1 vanilla bean, sliced in half

2 cups water

5 large eggs, 4 whole plus 1 yolk

Note: *Always* wear protection on your hands and keep children and pets out of the kitchen when working with hot caramel.

1. Pour 2 cups sugar in a wide sauté pan and place over low heat for about 10 minutes. Do not stir the sugar. At most, pick up the pan and swish it around to make sure the sugar is evenly melting. As soon as almost all of the sugar has turned to caramel, turn off the heat.

2. Working with one ramekin at a time, pour some caramel into the bottom and, with an oven glove–covered hand, swirl the ramekin so that the caramel coats about half of the inside. Repeat with five other ramekins. Work quickly as the caramel in the pan will also be cooling. Set aside.

3. In a heavy-bottomed saucepan, heat milk and vanilla bean over medium heat. Stir occasionally until the mixture begins to bubble. Turn off the heat and let cool (about 20–30 minutes). Remove the vanilla bean and scrape the seeds into the mixture.

4. In the meantime, prepare the pressure cooker by filling it with water and inserting the trivet or steamer basket.

5. In a mixing bowl, whisk the eggs and yolk and ²/₃ cup granulated sugar until the sugar is dissolved. Slowly pour in the cooled milk mixture and incorporate it into the yolks. Whisk lightly, but do not whip the mixture.

6. Pour mixture into the prepared ramekins, cover with foil, and arrange in steamer basket so that all are sitting straight. You can stack some of the cups on top in a second layer. Close and lock the lid.

7. Turn the heat up to high. When the cooker reaches pressure, lower the heat to the minimum needed to maintain pressure. Cook for 5–8 minutes at high pressure.

8. Open with the natural release method—move the pressure cooker to a cool burner and wait for the pressure to come down on its own (about 10 minutes). For electric pressure cookers, disengage the "keep warm" mode or unplug the cooker. After 10 minutes, release the rest of the pressure using the valve.

9. Open the pressure cooker and carefully lift out the custards. Open the first and jiggle it a bit. It should be nearly solid (they will solidify further when chilled). Remove the custards and leave to cool uncovered for about 30–45 minutes. Then, cover with plastic wrap and refrigerate for 3–24 hours.

10. To serve, run a skewer around the edge of each ramekin and flip upside down on a dessert plate.

Vanilla Pot de Crème

Serves 6

1 cup whole milk
1 cup heavy cream
1 vanilla bean, halved
2 cups water
1 teaspoon vegetable oil
6 egg yolks
²/₃ cup granulated sugar

1. In a heavy-bottomed saucepan, heat milk, cream, and vanilla bean over medium heat. Stir occasionally until the mixture begins to bubble.

2. Turn off the heat and let cool (about 20–30 minutes). Remove the vanilla bean and scrape the seeds into the mixture.

3. In the meantime, prepare the pressure cooker by filling it with water and inserting the trivet or steamer basket. Oil six teacups or ramekins.

4. In a mixing bowl, whisk the egg yolks and granulated sugar until the sugar is dissolved.

5. Slowly pour in the cooled milk mixture and incorporate it into the yolks. Whisk lightly, but do not whip the mixture.

6. Pour mixture into cups, cover with foil, and arrange in steamer basket so that all are sitting straight. You can stack some of the cups on top in a second layer. Close and lock the lid.

7. Turn the heat up to high. When the cooker reaches pressure, lower the heat to the minimum needed to maintain pressure. Cook for 8–10 minutes at high pressure.

8. Open with the natural release method—move the pressure cooker to a cool burner and wait for the pressure to come down on its own (about 10 minutes). For electric pressure cookers, disengage the "keep warm" mode or unplug the cooker. After 10 minutes, release the rest of the pressure using the valve.

9. Open the pressure cooker and carefully lift out the custards. Open the first and jiggle it a bit. It should be nearly solid (they will solidify further when chilled). Remove the custards and leave to cool uncovered for about 30–45 minutes. Then, cover with plastic wrap and refrigerate for 3–24 hours before serving.

Coconut Rice

Serves 6

1 tablespoon butter

2 cups extra-long-grain white rice, rinsed and drained

1/2 cup flaked or grated unsweetened coconut

3 cups water

1/4 cup currants

1/2 teaspoon ground cinnamon

1 teaspoon anise seeds

1/8 teaspoon ground cloves

1/2 teaspoon salt

1. Heat butter in an uncovered pressure cooker over medium heat. Sauté the rice, stirring well to coat it in the butter. Add the coconut, water, currants, cinnamon, anise seeds, cloves, and salt. Close and lock the lid.

2. Turn the heat up to high. When the cooker reaches pressure, lower the heat to the minimum needed to maintain pressure. Cook for 3 minutes at high pressure.

3. Open with the natural release method—move the pressure cooker to a cool burner and wait for the pressure to come down on its own (about 10 minutes). For electric pressure cookers, disengage the "keep warm" mode or unplug the cooker. After 10 minutes, release the rest of the pressure using the valve.

4. Fluff with a fork and serve.

Jennadene's Ricotta Cake

Serves 6

1 pound ricotta cheese

2 eggs

2 tablespoons granulated sugar

¼ cup honey

Zest and juice of ½ orange

¼ teaspoon vanilla extract

½ cup dates, soaked for 20 minutes, drained, and finely chopped

2 cups water

1. Beat ricotta until smooth, then set aside.

2. In a separate bowl or food processor, beat the eggs and sugar for 3 minutes. Combine the egg mixture with the ricotta.

3. In a small saucepan, warm the honey and whisk in orange juice, vanilla, and orange zest.

4. Stir the honey mixture into the ricotta mixture and add the chopped dates. Mix well for at least a few minutes to distribute the dates and create a smooth batter.

5. Pour into a buttered heatproof dish and cover with foil.

6. Prepare the pressure cooker by filling it with water and inserting the trivet or steamer basket. Make a foil sling by folding a long piece of foil into three and lower the covered dish into the pressure cooker. Close and lock the lid.

7. Turn the heat up to high. When the cooker reaches pressure, lower the heat to the minimum needed to maintain pressure. Cook for 22–25 minutes at high pressure.

8. When time is up, open the pressure cooker by quick-releasing the pressure.

9. Serve warm or well chilled.

Molten Fudge Pudding Cake

Serves 6

4 ounces semisweet chocolate chips

¼ cup cocoa

⅛ teaspoon salt

3 tablespoons butter, divided

2 large eggs, separated

¼ cup sugar, plus extra for the pan

1 teaspoon vanilla extract

½ cup pecans, chopped

¼ cup plus 2 tablespoons all-purpose flour

2 teaspoons instant coffee granules

2 tablespoons coffee liqueur

1 cup water

1. Add the chocolate chips, cocoa, salt, and 2 tablespoons butter to a microwave-safe bowl. Microwave on high for 1 minute; stir well. Microwave in additional 20-second segments if necessary, until the butter and chocolate are melted. Set aside to cool.

2. Add the egg whites to a medium-sized mixing bowl. Whisk or beat with a handheld mixer until the egg whites are foamy. Gradually add the ¼ cup of sugar, continuing to whisk or beat until soft peaks form; set aside.

3. Add the egg yolks and vanilla to a mixing bowl; use a whisk or handheld mixer to beat until the yolks are light yellow and begin to stiffen. Stir in the cooled chocolate mixture, pecans, flour, instant coffee, and coffee liqueur.

4. Transfer a third of the beaten egg whites to the chocolate mixture; stir to loosen the batter. Gently fold in the remaining egg whites.

5. Treat the bottom and sides of a 1-quart metal pan with 2 teaspoons of the remaining butter. Add about a tablespoon of sugar to the pan; shake and roll to coat the buttered pan with the sugar.

6. Dump out and discard any extra sugar. Transfer the chocolate batter to the buttered pan.

Molten Fudge Pudding Cake—continued

7. Treat one side of a 15" piece of aluminum foil with the remaining teaspoon of butter. Place the foil butter side down over the top of the pan; crimp around the edges of the pan to form a seal.

8. Pour the water into the pressure cooker. Place the rack in the cooker. Create handles to use later to remove the pan by crisscrossing long, doubled strips of foil over the rack.

9. Place the metal pan in the center of the rack over the foil strips. Lock the lid into place and bring to low pressure; maintain pressure for 20 minutes.

10. Remove pressure cooker from heat, quick-release pressure, and remove the lid. Lift the pan out of the pressure cooker and place on a wire rack. Remove foil cover.

11. Let rest for 10–15 minutes. To serve, either spoon from the pan or run a knife around the edge of the pan, place a serving plate over the metal pan, and invert to transfer the cake.

Glazed Lemon Poppy Seed Cake

Chapter 12: Sweets and Desserts

Glazed Lemon Poppy Seed Cake

Serves 8

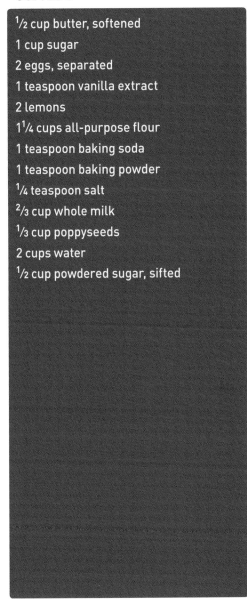

½ cup butter, softened

1 cup sugar

2 eggs, separated

1 teaspoon vanilla extract

2 lemons

1¼ cups all-purpose flour

1 teaspoon baking soda

1 teaspoon baking powder

¼ teaspoon salt

⅔ cup whole milk

⅓ cup poppyseeds

2 cups water

½ cup powdered sugar, sifted

1. Add the butter and sugar to a mixing bowl; beat until light and fluffy. Beat in the egg yolks, vanilla, grated zest from 1 lemon, and juice from 1 lemon.

2. Mix together the flour, baking soda, baking powder, and salt. Add the flour and milk in 3 batches to the butter mixture, mixing after each addition. Stir in the poppy seeds.

3. Add the egg whites to a chilled bowl. Whisk or beat until stiff. Fold the egg whites into the poppy seed batter.

4. Treat a 4-cup soufflé dish or Bundt pan with nonstick spray. Transfer the batter to the pan. Treat a 15" square of heavy-duty aluminum foil with nonstick spray. Place the foil, treated side down, over the pan; crimp around the edges to seal.

5. Pour the water and place the rack into the pressure cooker. Crisscross long, doubled strips of foil over the rack to create handles to use later to remove the pan.

6. Place the pan on the rack over the foil strips. Lock the lid into place and bring to low pressure; maintain pressure for 40 minutes.

7. Remove from heat and allow pressure to release naturally. Remove the lid. Lift the pan from the pressure cooker and place it on a cooling rack. Remove foil cover.

8. To make the glaze, whisk the juice and grated zest from the remaining lemon together with the powdered sugar. Transfer the cake to a serving platter and drizzle the glaze over the top.

Molten Chocolate Mug Cake

Serves 1

4 tablespoons flour

¼ teaspoon orange zest

4 tablespoons sugar

⅛ teaspoon salt

1 tablespoon unsweetened cocoa powder

½ teaspoon baking powder

1 medium egg

4 tablespoons milk

2 tablespoons extra-virgin olive oil

2 cups water

1. In a medium-sized mug, add the flour, orange zest, sugar, salt, cocoa powder, and baking powder and mix with a fork.

2. In a small bowl, beat the egg, milk, and olive oil. Pour egg mixture into mug and mix vigorously until smooth.

3. Prepare the pressure cooker by filling it with water and inserting the trivet or steamer basket. Lower the uncovered mug into the pressure cooker. Close and lock the lid.

4. Turn the heat up to high. When the cooker reaches pressure, lower the heat to the minimum needed to maintain pressure. Cook for 5–8 minutes at high pressure.

5. When time is up, open the pressure cooker by quick-releasing the pressure.

6. Carefully remove mug and serve immediately. Poke the top of the cake to release steam and stop the molten center from cooking further.

Spiced Chocolate Cake

Serves 10–12

1½ cups all-purpose flour

4 tablespoons cocoa powder

1 teaspoon cinnamon

1 teaspoon cayenne pepper

1 teaspoon sugar

¼ teaspoon salt

1 teaspoon baking powder

2 large eggs, beaten, or 2 mashed bananas

4 tablespoons butter, melted, or vegan margarine, such as Earth Balance

1 cup milk, or soymilk

2 cups hot water

1. In a medium bowl, mix the flour, cocoa powder, cinnamon, cayenne, sugar, salt, and baking powder. In a large bowl, beat the eggs. Add the dry ingredients to the eggs. Slowly stir in the melted butter and the milk. Pour the cake mixture into an 8" round pan.

2. Add the steaming rack to the pressure cooker and pour in the hot water. Place the cake in the pressure cooker and lock the lid into place. Bring to high pressure, then reduce to low and cook for 30 minutes.

3. Remove the pressure cooker from the heat, quick-release the steam, and carefully remove the cake.

Banana Pudding Cake

Serves 12

1 (18$\frac{1}{4}$-ounce) package yellow cake mix, or vegan cake mix

1 (3$\frac{1}{2}$-ounce) package instant banana pudding mix, or vegan pudding mix

4 large eggs, or 4 ounces silken tofu

4 cups water, divided

$\frac{1}{4}$ cup vegetable oil

3 small ripe bananas, mashed

2 cups powdered sugar, sifted

2 tablespoons milk, or soymilk

1 teaspoon vanilla extract

$\frac{1}{2}$ cup walnuts, toasted and chopped

1. Treat a 1-quart or 6-cup Bundt or angel food cake pan with nonstick spray. Set aside.

2. Add the cake mix and pudding mix to a large mixing bowl; stir to mix. Make a well in the center and add the eggs and pour in 1 cup water, oil, and mashed banana.

3. Beat on low speed until blended. Scrape bowl and beat another 4 minutes on medium speed. Pour the batter into the prepared pan. Cover tightly with a piece of heavy-duty aluminum foil.

4. Pour 3 cups water into the pressure cooker and add the rack. Lower the cake pan onto the rack.

5. Lock the lid into place and bring to high pressure; maintain pressure for 35 minutes.

6. Remove the pressure cooker from the heat, quick-release the pressure, and remove the lid.

7. Lift the cake pan out of the pressure cooker and place on a wire rack to cool for 10 minutes, then turn the cake out onto the wire rack to finish cooling.

8. To make the glaze, mix together the powdered sugar, milk, and vanilla in a bowl. Drizzle over the top of the cooled cake. Sprinkle the walnuts over the glaze before the glaze dries.

Metric Conversion Chart

VOLUME CONVERSIONS

U.S. Volume Measure	Metric Equivalent
⅛ teaspoon	0.5 milliliter
¼ teaspoon	1 milliliter
½ teaspoon	2 milliliters
1 teaspoon	5 milliliters
½ tablespoon	7 milliliters
1 tablespoon (3 teaspoons)	15 milliliters
2 tablespoons (1 fluid ounce)	30 milliliters
¼ cup (4 tablespoons)	60 milliliters
⅓ cup	90 milliliters
½ cup (4 fluid ounces)	125 milliliters
⅔ cup	160 milliliters
¾ cup (6 fluid ounces)	180 milliliters
1 cup (16 tablespoons)	250 milliliters
1 pint (2 cups)	500 milliliters
1 quart (4 cups)	1 liter (about)

WEIGHT CONVERSIONS

U.S. Weight Measure	Metric Equivalent
½ ounce	15 grams
1 ounce	30 grams
2 ounces	60 grams
3 ounces	85 grams
¼ pound (4 ounces)	115 grams
½ pound (8 ounces)	225 grams
¾ pound (12 ounces)	340 grams
1 pound (16 ounces)	454 grams

OVEN TEMPERATURE CONVERSIONS

Degrees Fahrenheit	Degrees Celsius
200 degrees F	95 degrees C
250 degrees F	120 degrees C
275 degrees F	135 degrees C
300 degrees F	150 degrees C
325 degrees F	160 degrees C
350 degrees F	180 degrees C
375 degrees F	190 degrees C
400 degrees F	205 degrees C
425 degrees F	220 degrees C
450 degrees F	230 degrees C

BAKING PAN SIZES

American	Metric
8 x 1½ inch round baking pan	20 x 4 cm cake tin
9 x 1½ inch round baking pan	23 x 3.5 cm cake tin
11 x 7 x 1½ inch baking pan	28 x 18 x 4 cm baking tin
13 x 9 x 2 inch baking pan	30 x 20 x 5 cm baking tin
2 quart rectangular baking dish	30 x 20 x 3 cm baking tin
15 x 10 x 2 inch baking pan	30 x 25 x 2 cm baking tin (Swiss roll tin)
9 inch pie plate	22 x 4 or 23 x 4 cm pie plate
7 or 8 inch springform pan	18 or 20 cm springform or loose bottom cake tin
9 x 5 x 3 inch loaf pan	23 x 13 x 7 cm or 2 lb narrow loaf or pate tin
1½ quart casserole	1.5 liter casserole
2 quart casserole	2 liter casserole

Index

Note: Page numbers in **bold** indicate recipe category lists at a glance.
Page numbers in *italics* indicate photographs.